PUBLIC SCHOLARSHIP IN DANCE

Teaching, Choreography, Research, Service, and Assessment for Community Engagement

Lynnette Young Overby, PhD

University of Delaware

HUMAN KINETICS

Library of Congress Cataloging-in-Publication Data

Overby, Lynnette Young.
  Public scholarship in dance : teaching, choreography, research, service, and assessment for community engagement / Lynnette Young Overby, PhD, University of Delaware.
    pages cm
  1. Dance--Study and teaching. 2. Choreography--Study and teaching. 3. Dance--Social aspects. 4. Learning and scholarship. 5. Community development. I. Title.
  GV1589.O84 2016
  792.807--dc23
                                    2015013551
  ISBN: 978-1-4504-2438-7 (print)

Acquisitions Editor: Gayle Kassing, PhD; **Developmental Editor:** Melissa Feld; **Managing Editor:** Derek Campbell; **Copyeditor:** Jan Feeney; **Permissions Manager:** Dalene Reeder; **Graphic Designer:** Dawn Sills; **Cover Designer:** Keith Blomberg; **Photographers (cover):** © Zero Creatives/agefotostock (dancers) and Art Explosion (background); **Photo Asset Manager:** Laura Fitch; **Visual Production Assistant:** Joyce Brumfield; **Photo Production Manager:** Jason Allen; **Art Manager:** Kelly Hendren; **Associate Art Manager:** Alan L. Wilborn; **Illustrations:** © Human Kinetics, unless otherwise noted; **Printer:** Versa Press

Printed in the United States of America   10 9 8 7 6 5 4 3 2 1

The paper in this book is certified under a sustainable forestry program.

Human Kinetics
Website: www.HumanKinetics.com

United States: Human Kinetics
P.O. Box 5076
Champaign, IL 61825-5076
800-747-4457
e-mail: humank@hkusa.com

Canada: Human Kinetics
475 Devonshire Road Unit 100
Windsor, ON N8Y 2L5
800-465-7301 (in Canada only)
e-mail: info@hkcanada.com

Europe: Human Kinetics
107 Bradford Road
Stanningley
Leeds LS28 6AT, United Kingdom
+44 (0) 113 255 5665
e-mail: hk@hkeurope.com

Australia: Human Kinetics
57A Price Avenue
Lower Mitcham, South Australia 5062
08 8372 0999
e-mail: info@hkaustralia.com

New Zealand: Human Kinetics
P.O. Box 80
Mitcham Shopping Centre, South Australia 5062
0800 222 062
e-mail: info@hknewzealand.com

E5659

I dedicate this book to my husband Cordell, my children Collin and Casey, my parents James and Susan Young, and my parents-in-law James and Mildred Overby. Without your unconditional love and support, this project, and many others, would not have been possible.

To my dancing friends and colleagues from Hampton, Washington, DC, Maryland, Michigan, and Delaware and members of the National Dance Association, National Dance Education Organization, Michigan Dance Council, and Dance and the Child International—thank you for sharing your friendship and knowledge with me.

To my ArtsBridge Scholars from Michigan State University and University of Delaware, thank you for your dedication to making a difference in the lives of students through arts integration—I have learned a great deal from you.

Finally, I dedicate this book to the many dance and K-12 teachers and students for continuing to inspire me to co-create mutually enriching dance experiences.

Thank you very much.

CONTENTS

Preface   vii

1 What Is Public Scholarship in Dance?   1

2 Teaching   19

3 Choreography   37

4 Research   55

5 Service   77

6 Assessment   91

7 Final Thoughts   99

Appendix   105
Bibliography   123
Resources   127
About the Author   132
Contributor List   133

PREFACE

Dance educators in higher education settings have extended their reach into the community through various routes, including teaching, choreography, research, and service—and they have made a difference. Through public scholarship, dance education transcends the traditional university-based teaching, choreography, research, and service and yields positive outcomes for students, the larger community, and most important the dance professors. However, a focus on community work can sometimes cause problems when traversing the minefields of merit, promotion, and tenure in the university.

This book is a resource for the development, implementation, and assessment of community projects for budding and experienced dance scholars who have chosen to incorporate community engagement in their lives. Although the majority of the examples in this book are from universities in the United States, the topic of public scholarship (also known as community engagement) is not limited to the United States. Many international universities are affiliated with a range of community engagement organizations. Examples are the Global Alliance on Community-Engaged Research and the Asia Pacific University Engagement Network. Each of these organizations provides opportunities for networking, professional development, publications, and presentations.

My foray into public scholarship began with a simple question: Given the state of dance education in the United States, where dance education occurs primarily in private schools of dance, how can we give more people access to this art form? Dance is the art form K-12 students have the least opportunity to experience, whereas students are able to study visual art and music in most public schools. Because of this inequity, I vigorously pursued a variety of approaches that began to merge my teaching, research, and service into a form of scholarship that views the community as a rich resource for collaboration and enabled me to develop several strategies that provide dance experiences for many more students through arts integration and performance.

Throughout this book you will hear the voices of higher education dance professionals in the United States and beyond who have navigated the waters of higher education as public scholars. They allow you to explore their journey—the triumphs and trials—as they enrich the lives of students, communities, and the discipline.

Public Scholarship in Dance contains specific models that serve as guides in the development, implementation, and assessment of dance projects developed by university dance educators. Although the strategies can apply to dance educators in other settings, the goal of this publication is to assist university dance educators in creating scholarly community-focused projects. The book is therefore divided into the stated missions of higher education—teaching, research, and service; for dance educators the category of choreography is added.

This book is organized into seven chapters and includes an appendix and resources.

• **Chapter 1 What Is Public Scholarship in Dance?** A brief history of public scholarship in higher education is presented. Kolb's theory of experiential learning is used as a guide. The model supports the learning that will take place among all partners: dance educator, students, and community partner.

Kolb's theory has been used as a way to visualize and comprehend learning. It speaks to the cyclical, reflective nature of cognition with a goal of engaging individuals in an active process of learning. In each of the processes—teaching, research, and choreography—Kolb's theory of experiential learning provides a structure for planning, implementing, and assessing these cognitive activities that rely on active experimentation.

The work of public scholars is process oriented and experiential, a university- and community-centered approach to learning. Learning is the process whereby knowledge is created through the transformation of experience (Kolb 1984). The chapter concludes with several additional models, including the public scholarship in dance quadrant.

• **Chapter 2 Teaching.** Academic service learning provides dance educators with the opportunity to focus on the experiential learning needs of students. As a high-impact practice that has been proven to promote student engagement and retention (Kuh 2008), academic service learning is becoming more prevalent in the academy in all disciplines, including the teaching of dance.

• **Chapter 3 Choreography.** Choreography lends itself nicely to community expression as a reflection of the lives of people, places, and societal problems. The experiences of university-based choreographers are profiled in this chapter. Guidelines for the development and assessment of community-based choreography are revealed.

• **Chapter 4 Research.** Research is the keystone of a career in higher education. Becoming deeply informed in the discipline and moving it forward through the rigorous, systematic exploration of a topic continue to be the basis of survival in higher education. When research moves beyond the walls of the university and communities become integral to the design, implementation, and dissemination of this research, a career in public scholarship has begun to take shape. Additional research methodologies are included in this chapter.

• **Chapter 5 Service.** In a traditional university setting, service is often given the least amount of weight in decisions on tenure and promotion. Service is looked at broadly as committee work at the university level, including serving on panels and editing journals. This chapter makes a case for service as scholarship by demonstrating how applying specific assessment criteria that demonstrate impact can make the difference between low-level and high-level scholarly service.

• **Chapter 6 Assessment.** Various forms of assessments provide public scholars with materials that can be used for documentation of community engagement projects and for evaluation and revision of current work. Ongoing assessment is essential for marketing, documentation, and preparation of materials for considerations on promotion, tenure, and merit.

• **Chapter 7 Final Thoughts.** A review of the previous chapters provides a vision for the future of dance education, one that considers the community an integral part of the mission.

• **Appendix.** The appendix presents several templates that can be put to use in community-engaged teaching, research, service, and choreography.

• **Resources.** The decision to become a public scholar in dance and other disciplines has become easier because of the availability of resources. National organizations provide guidance and standards for scholarly work. They serve as a venue for publications and presentations. Furthermore, presentations by nationally recognized engaged scholars are motivating and engaging. This section of the book includes information about organizations, websites, books, journals, and other resources to guide the development, implementation, and dissemination of teaching, choreography, research, and service projects in public scholarship.

Public Scholarship in Dance provides a link from theory to practice with many real-life examples that inform the design and implementation of projects. The inspiration for this book comes from the gratification of seeing the positive impact of public scholarship on students and communities. In contrast, inspiration comes from the distress that accompanies public scholars whose work goes unrewarded and unrecognized because it fails to fit into the traditional realm of higher education. My wish is that all dance faculty members who desire to contribute to the greater good through their lives in academia can do so and know that their work is valued.

1

WHAT IS PUBLIC SCHOLARSHIP IN DANCE?

Dance professors must collect evidence that is empirical enough to prove that what they do is real, that it is scholarship, and that it is worthy of merit in academic terms. In academic environments, the problem with public scholarship as it is applied to dance is that it must dance.

Ella Magruder, *Dancing for Young Audiences*

Public scholarship is academic inquiry that forms community part-nerships to address shared problems, issues, and opportunities. *Public scholarship, scholarship of engagement, community-engaged scholarship,* and *community engagement* are terms used interchangeably to redefine faculty scholarly work from application of academic expertise to com-munity-engaged scholarship involving a faculty member in a reciprocal partnership with the community. Public scholarship integrates faculty roles of teaching, research, and service in collaboration with individuals outside the academy. These individuals are knowledge professionals and the lay public (local, regional or state, national, global) involved in a mutually beneficial exchange of knowledge and resources in a context of partnership and reciprocity.

Public scholars are faculty members who apply their disciplinary lens to opportunities and challenges in a community setting. The focus very often begins with knowledge of a societal problem. Scholars with unique disciplinary expertise then apply this knowledge to their teaching (curricular community engagement, including academic ser-vice learning), research (community based), choreography, or service (external to the university). The projects that result from this focus are co-created, co-implemented, and co-assessed with community partners. Dance educators in higher education are often involved in important services such as the development of state and national edu-cational standards, assessments, and curriculum development. Com-munity-focused teaching may include service learning classes, where students apply their knowledge of dance in a school or community setting or in research that explores the impact of learning dance on youth empowerment or through choreography, as a touring company introduces an audience of third-grade students to life in various cur-ricular connections through dance.

This chapter presents a brief history of public scholarship and com-munity engagement in higher education. Next is a discussion of public scholarship through dance. Finally, a theoretical framework and engage-ment models are advanced to set the stage for the chapters that follow.

BRIEF HISTORY OF PUBLIC SCHOLARSHIP IN HIGHER EDUCATION

American universities have been linked to their communities since the 1700s. The early American colonial colleges and universities were very much like the early European universities. There existed a pri-marily scholastic curriculum, with some strong humanist influences.

Three "liberal" studies were in use at the time of the founding of the colonial colleges: a residue of the scholastic classical program, with emphasis on logic; *studia humanitatis*, generally in deteriorated form and compromised by scholasticism, including a reliance on classical languages and literature taught by dry grammatical and rhetorical rules; and liberal-free subjects, primarily natural and experimental sciences and modern languages (Kimball, quoted in Dirks 1996). The classical curriculum was designed to develop minds through the study of Latin, philosophy, and metaphysics. There was also very little specific disciplinary teaching until 1825 when Harvard opened the door for disciplinary specialization by allowing students to select a major (Dirks 1996).

The Organic Act of 1837 established the University of Michigan as a public university, separating the mission from that of the liberal colonial colleges. Unlike the traditional colonial and European colleges that focused on learning Greek, Latin, rhetoric, grammar, and philosophy and recitations and memorization as means of assessment, Michigan followed the tradition of the German universities, which had become the best in the world by including lectures, seminars, laboratories, and a clear focus on teaching and research.

By 1862, President Lincoln signed the Morrill Act, which led to the founding of the first land-grant universities. These universities had a mandate for serving the public. Other acts (the Hatch Act of 1887 and the Smith-Lever Act of 1914) established the agriculture extension focus of universities, and in 1890 the Morrill Act expanded to include 70 colleges that became known as the HBCUs (historically black colleges and universities). In 1992, Hispanic-serving institutions were formally recognized, and in 1994 funding was provided to establish a system of tribal colleges and universities (Fitzgerald 2010). With these historic changes in higher education, the United States began to embed applied research and scholarship in publically supported institutions of higher learning.

EXPANDING THE DEFINITION OF SCHOLARSHIP

Although land-grant universities began to appear, the research purposes of universities started to take hold. By the end of the 19th century, scientific objectivity was the expectation of all professors (Hartley and Harkavy 2010). The research focus of most universities continued through the mid-1980s.

In the mid-1980s, presidents from Brown, Stanford, and Georgetown Universities founded the Campus Compact. This organization helped students make a difference through public and community service (Glass and Fitzgerald 2010). During that period, a prominent voice began to change the landscape of higher education: Ernest Boyer.

Boyer, president of the Carnegie Foundation for the Advancement of Teaching, was disappointed by the singular focus on research accompanied by the lack of attention to undergraduate education at many universities. Thus, he encouraged an expansion of the definition of scholarship to include four domains: teaching, discovery, integration, and application (Boyer 1990). Shortly before his untimely death, he expanded on the scholarship of application by using the term *engagement*:

> *The academy must become a more vigorous partner in the search of answers to our most pressing social, civic, economic, and moral problems, and must reaffirm its historic commitment to what I call the scholarship of engagement. (Boyer 1996, p. 11)*

The four areas reflect both the academic and civic components of faculty work and promote a deeper commitment to the full range of scholarship. The scholarship of discovery is the traditional path of research. Researchers pursue new knowledge, a critical mission of faculty in higher education.

Faculty involved in the scholarship of integration make connections across disciplines. By conducting and interpreting research that crosses disciplines, new insights are revealed. The scholarship of teaching refers to teaching—not merely lecturing—that transmits, transforms, and extends knowledge. The teacher is steeped in disciplinary knowledge and transmits that knowledge in a way that provokes students to think critically and creatively.

Finally, the scholarship of application or engagement applies and contributes to human knowledge. Engaged faculty members are involved in activities that flow directly from their scholarship. This is not a service activity that too often is categorized as just doing good, but a rigorous, thoughtful extension of disciplinary scholarship in contributing new knowledge to a local, regional, or global problem. Faculty members conduct engaged scholarship in partnership with community members in a mutually beneficial manner.

In response to Boyer's writing, many universities looked closely at their mission statements and the singular focus on research as the dominating force of the university and made significant changes. For example, Michigan State University has been a leader in committing resources for the acceptance of scholarly engagement. Beginning in the early 1990s the university convened faculty who developed criteria for the assessment of outreach and engagement projects. They have continued to lead the way in the creation of documents that have influenced many other universities. Of course, change in a singular focus on research requires commitment from administration, faculty, students, community members, and disciplinary organizations.

Scholarship Assessed (1997), published after Boyer's death, provides a means of evaluation for the four domains of scholarship and includes a means of assessment based on rigorous standards. Throughout the book are clear recommendations for the assessment of all scholarly work, including teaching and engagement. The project (teaching, discovery, integrative, or engaged) should include clear goals, adequate preparation, appropriate methods, significant results, effective presentation, and reflective critique (Glassick, Huber, and Maeroff 1997). A focus on standards for all types of scholarship allowed universities to begin to look more closely at the criteria for merit, promotion, and tenure. Several universities began the task of changing standards and changing a culture by having guidelines and criteria in place for review committees and faculty members. In this book, the assessment criteria presented in *Scholarship Assessed* are applied to the dance projects in the service category.

Since the creation of the Campus Compact, and because of the influence of Ernest Boyer and other pioneers of the academic service learning movement, the number of universities with offices devoted to service learning and community engagement has grown. In a 1990 survey, only 15 percent of the member campuses had offices of service learning and civic engagement. In a 2010 survey, 95 percent of the member campuses had a central service learning office, and 90 percent of the institutions included engagement in their mission statements (Hartley 2012).

Another organization that has a positive impact on the community-engagement focus of higher education is Imagining America: Artists and Scholars in Public Life, a consortium of more than 70 colleges and universities. The consortium established a tenure team and developed a report that provides guidelines for the development and interpretation of public scholarship. The document, published in 2008 (Ellison and Eatman 2008), includes the following recommendations:

1. Define public scholarly and creative work.
2. Develop policy based on a continuum of scholarship.
3. Recognize the excellence of work that connects domains of knowledge.

4. Expand what counts.

5. Document what counts.

6. Present what counts: Use portfolios.

7. Expand who counts: Broaden the community of peer review.

8. Support publicly engaged graduate students and junior faculty.

9. Build in flexibility at the point of hire.

10. Promote public scholars to full professor.

11. Organize the department for policy change.

12. Take this report home and use it to start something.

Over time, the stated missions of many universities have evolved from a focus on research and teaching to a more inclusive focus on scholarly research, teaching, and engagement. Universities are increasingly invested in the needs and concerns of the larger community (Boyer 1990, 1996; Bloomgarden and O'Meara 2007; Campus Compact 2000). However, there is still a need to clarify methods for the development and implementation of scholarly engagement as well as a need for more openness to change by traditional faculty who often make decisions about merit, promotion, and tenure of the more community-engaged faculty members. This book provides guidelines on connecting public scholarship to dance.

COMMUNITY ENGAGEMENT IN DANCE AND HIGHER EDUCATION

Margaret H'Doubler at the University of Wisconsin established the first dance major in the United States in 1926. Currently, more than 200 degree-granting dance programs exist in the nation. Dance educators at those universities provide technical training and cultural, historical, and aesthetic content for dance students. University dance programs also provide a valuable performing and teaching service for the surrounding community. Although dance has become an important component of many universities, dance is still rarely represented in the K-12 school system. In fact, less than 3 percent of all schools in the United States have dance teachers (Aud et al. 2011).

Throughout the history of dance in higher education, educators have devoted time and resources to establishing dance as an art form. Many dance educators have also connected their scholarship with community partners. The chapters that follow provide examples of community engagement, including leading the development of state

Florin Prunoiu / age fotostock

Engaging in dance with community members is an important part of public scholarship in dance.

and national education standards and engaging the community as a performance venue.

Community dance programs are part of the curricula of many colleges, including historically black colleges and universities (HBCUs) (Overby, Tucker, and Terry-Todd 1992). Established as land-grant universities, the HBCUs have always been connected to their communities in many disciplines, including dance. Through community dance programs, the HBCUs extend their reach so that children in the surrounding communities can experience dance. For African American children growing up in segregated communities in the 1940s and 1950s, the HBCUs provided the few places they could study dance. Today, the community dance programs at many HBCUs, including Coppin State University, provide extensive course selection for their surrounding communities.

Moreover, dance programs throughout the United States provide an important service for the community. Dance Arizona Repertory Theatre (DART) is an example. DART is a dance program associated with Arizona State University that engages the community in long-term sustainable dance experiences. From 1998 to 2007, this program co-created dances with the Herrera School for the Fine Arts at Arizona State University and Boys and Girls Clubs of the Phoenix area.

7

University students highly skilled in dance technique collaborated with middle school youth from the inner city of Phoenix. Through the years, collaborations with students, faculty, professional choreographers, and the middle school students enhanced the learning of all parties. Interestingly, the description of this program in the book *Dance, Human Rights, and Social Justice* (Fitzgerald 2008) details the lack of value assigned to this type of work by the university. This program and others like it are primarily seen as a type of social service, not a scholarly endeavor.

Dance educators in higher education need continued support in their efforts to form collaborations with community partners through their teaching, choreography, and service. Evidence exists that demonstrates the effect of public scholarship on all parties: faculty, student, and community partner. Kelly Ward and Tami Moore (2007) of Washington State University describe these benefits in figure 1.1. Reflective practices are an indicator of learning that occurs in both students and faculty members. Reflective practices provide time and space for thinking critically about an experience. Reflections may take the form of journal prompts, drawings, and artistic interpretations.

MODELS AND THEORIES OF PUBLIC SCHOLARSHIP

Models and theories allow you to create engagement projects that are well crafted and address higher education administrators' concern for rigor and impact—impact that provides evidence for cases concerning merit, promotion, and tenure. The following models—Kolb's theory of experiential learning, the outreach and engagement continuum, and the public scholarship in dance quadrant—provide guidance for the development and assessment of projects that meet the level of rigor required for being deemed scholarly. Additional checklists for the development and assessment of public scholarship projects are in the appendix.

Kolb's Theory of Experiential Learning

Kolb's theory of experiential learning views learning as a process, not an outcome (see figure 1.2). The theory did not begin with Kolb; it is based on the work of John Dewey, Kurt Lewin, Jean Piaget, William James, Carl Jung, Paulo Freire, Carl Rogers, and other scholars (Kolb 1984; Turesky and Wood 2010). They each conducted research or tested

BENEFITS OF PUBLIC SCHOLARSHIP

Benefits to Faculty

- Reclaiming the role of the educator
- Blurring lines between teaching, research, and service when education is at the center
- Not limiting education to the classroom
- Pursuing passion
- Fueling faculty purpose through passion about community issues
- Making a difference in the lives of the community
- Maintaining passion through social justice orientation
- Gaining new understandings of disciplines and interdisciplinarity
- Working on margins of the university
- Securing grants to shift margins

Benefits to Students

- Experiencing real-world engagement
- Applying learning
- Exploring career paths
- Gaining pedagogy and class management skills
- Gaining research skills
- Gaining performance skills

Benefits to Communities

- Collaborating with the university to allow communities to find solutions to problems
- Gaining access to the rich resources of the university

Figure 1.1 Benefits of public scholarship for university faculty, students, and community partners based on research conducted by Kelly Ward and Tami Moore (2007).

theories about the power of experiences to transform learning and understanding. This form of learning encompasses a range of behaviors from a single performance to a long-term learning experience to lifelong development. "Learning is the process whereby knowledge is created through the transformation of experience" (Kolb 1984, p. 38).

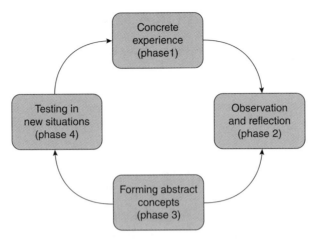

Figure 1.2 Kolb's experiential learning cycle.

Adapted from Learning Theories.com. Available: http://www.learning-theories.com/experiential-learning-kolb.html

Kolb's model comprises concrete experiences (or CE, which is phase 1), reflective observation (RO, phase 2), abstract conceptualization (AC, phase 3), and active experimentation (AE, phase 4). Phase 1 is the feeling stage. In this phase, the participants experience an activity. In phase 2, the watching phase, participants consciously reflect on the initial experience. In phase 3, the thinking phase, participants form abstract concepts by conceptualizing a model or theory based on the first two phases. In the final component, the doing stage, participants synthesize their knowledge and plan a new experience. This theory is adapted to dance throughout this book, providing guidance in the development and explanation of public scholarship in teaching, choreography, and research. Kolb's theory of experiential learning supports gains that will take place in all partners—dance educators, students, community partners, and universities.

The work of public scholars, in teaching service-learning courses or creating a dance work with a community partner, is process oriented and experiential—a community-centered approach to learning. This approach allows us to consciously and deliberately reflect on concrete experiences and transform and apply those experiences into new forms of knowledge (Turesky and Wood 2010). Table 1.1 displays specific examples of Kolb's model applied to dance scholarship. This format is used throughout the book with specific examples from teaching,

TABLE 1.1 Kolb's Experiential Learning Model With Examples From Dance Scholarship

Kolb's model	Actions	Outcomes
TEACHING: ACADEMIC SERVICE LEARNING		
Phase 1 Concrete experiences	Teacher provides many concrete examples of service learning.	Interdisciplinary dance course: Experience many examples of arts-integrated lessons.
Phase 2 Observation and reflection	Observe and reflect.	Go to a school and observe and reflect.
Phase 3 Forming abstract concepts	Design activities based on experiences and observations.	In collaboration with mentor or teacher, create several arts-integrated lessons.
Phase 4 Testing in new situations	Actively engage in applying learning in a new environment.	Teach and reflect on lessons.
Dissemination	Create reflective essays, posters, interviews, off-campus presentations, websites, journal articles, dance, drama, visual art, or music.	Complete an exit survey, write a reflective essay, and construct a poster.
RESEARCH		
Phase 1 Concrete experiences	Meet with community partner to discuss needs and read current research.	Professional development research: Meet with teachers to discuss needs and read current professional development and arts education research.
Phase 2 Observation and reflection	Observe situation, review pertinent research, and reflect on ability to apply knowledge.	Begin developing ideas about professional development in arts integration.

(continued)

Table 1.1 *(continued)*

Kolb's model	Actions	Outcomes
Phase 3 Forming abstract concepts	Develop a proposal in collaboration with community partner; complete a logic model.	Create a logic model and proposal based on best practices of professional development.
Phase 4 Testing in new situations	Conduct research, collect data, and focus on qualitative and quantitative outcomes.	Implement professional development training and collect and analyze data.
Dissemination	Write a journal article or book or make a presentation.	Write a journal article or book and present data nationally and internationally in arts dance education venues.
CHOREOGRAPHY		
Phase 1 Concrete experiences	Review similar community-based choreographic models.	Create a dance about a current issue. Review issue-based drama and dance choreography.
Phase 2 Observation and reflection	Discuss and try out ideas with community partners and students.	Meet with students and teachers; interview students and community members.
Phase 3 Forming abstract concepts	Create short studies in collaboration with community partners and students; share and revise.	Create short studies that depict problems and solutions, get feedback, revise.
Phase 4 Testing in new situations	Create new work, and develop appropriate assessments.	Create entire work with formative and summative assessment.
Dissemination	Share work through technology and other means to multiple publics.	Submit a journal article about the process, develop DVD, and upload on YouTube.

research, and choreography. Dissemination, an important component of public scholarship, is added to the table. Dissemination provides evidence of the many ways in which dance professionals share their work with the world. The examples in chapter 5, Service, occur in a different format. These examples use the assessment model of clear goals, adequate preparation, appropriate methods, significant results, effective presentation, and reflective critique (Glassick, Huber, and Maeroff 1997). Both Kolb's model and the assessment format in the book *Scholarship Assessed* enable dance educators to view and create their work in a scholarly manner.

Outreach and Engagement Continuum

The outreach and engagement continuum is based on the Michigan State University definition of outreach and engagement: a framework that is applicable to a variety of disciplines, including dance. Table 1.2 includes many examples of engagement activities that can be categorized under teaching, research, and service. According to Brown (2006), the best community engagement occurs when knowledge is co-generated, co-disseminated, co-preserved, and co-applied. Although all projects will not meet this standard, the continuum is a tool for the development and assessment of projects. No longer is it appropriate to only reach out to the community; you must engage with your community as partners. The outreach and engagement continuum provides examples that promote co-equal creation of knowledge. The continuum may be used in the design and evaluation of a scholarly engaged project.

Public Scholarship in Dance Quadrant (PSDQ)

The public scholarship in dance quadrant presents examples of projects that demonstrate a continuum of low to high scholarship (i.e., disciplinary knowledge) and low to high engagement (i.e., partnerships between community and university). Dance-related projects and activities at a high level are not merely disseminated but collaboratively created, implemented, and disseminated. The chart in figure 1.3 builds on the previous models, especially the outreach and engagement continuum. The chart contains examples of projects in each of the four quadrants: teaching, choreography, research, and service. This PSDQ is applied to projects described in later chapters.

Checklists also allow the project creator to ensure the successful development of public scholarship projects. These checklists are in appendixes A.1 to A.4.

TABLE 1.2 Outreach and Engagement Continuum

KD = Knowledge disseminated
KA = Knowledge applied
KD,A = Knowledge disseminated and applied
KG,D,A = Knowledge generated, disseminated, and applied
KG,D,P,A = Knowledge generated, disseminated, preserved, and applied
KcD = Knowledge co-disseminated
KcA = Knowledge co-applied
KcD,cA = Knowledge co-disseminated and co-applied
KcG,cD,cA = Knowledge co-generated, co-disseminated, and co-applied
KcG,cD,cP,cA = Knowledge co-generated, co-disseminated, co-preserved, and co-applied

Mission	Type	OUTREACH						ENGAGEMENT			
		KD	KA	KD,A	KG,D,A	KG,D,P,A	KcD	KcA	KcD,cA	KcG,cD,cA	KcG,cD,cP,cA
Research, discovery, creative works	Applied research				x	x				x	x
	Community-based research					x				x	x
	Contractual research				x	x				x	x
	Demonstration projects	x		x			x		x		
	Exhibitions and performances	x					x				
	Needs assessments and evaluation				x	x				x	x
	Knowledge transfer and research			x	x				x	x	
	Technical assistance		x								
	Publications and presentations					x					x

		OUTREACH AND ENGAGEMENT ANCHORED IN KNOWLEDGE MODEL									
		OUTREACH					ENGAGEMENT				
Mission	Type	KD	KA	KD,A	KG,D,A	KG,D,P,A	KcD	KcA	KcD,cA	KcG,cD, cA	KcG,cD, cP,cA
Teaching and learning	Service learning		x	x	x			x	x	x	
	Study abroad programs		x	x	x						
	Distance education and off-campus instruction	x					x				
	Continuing education	x					x				
	Contract courses or programs for specific audiences	x					x				
	Conferences, seminars, and workshops	x					x				
	Educational programs for alumni	x					x				
	Participatory curriculum development						x				

(continued)

Table 1.2 *(continued)*

Mission	Type	OUTREACH AND ENGAGEMENT ANCHORED IN KNOWLEDGE MODEL									
		OUTREACH						ENGAGEMENT			
		KD	KA	KD,A	KG,D,A	KG,D,P,A	KcD	KcA	KcD,cA	KcG,cD, cA	KcG,cD, cP,cA
Service and citizenship	Clinical services		X					X			
	Consulting		X								
	Policy analysis		X					X			
	Service to community-based institutions		X								
	Knowledge transfer and workshops		X					X			
	Expert testimony		X					X			
	Technical assistance		X								
	Contributions to managed systems		X					X			
	Leading professional societies and associations		X					X			
	Commercialization of discoveries		X	X	X	X		X	X	X	X
	New business ventures		X	X	X	X		X	X	X	X

FIGURE 1.3 PUBLIC SCHOLARSHIP IN DANCE QUADRANT

High scholarship, low engagement	High scholarship, high engagement
Teaching: Teach dance history to students **Research:** Test the effects of strength training on dance performance **Choreography and Performance:** Perform a new dance work based on a painting **Service**: Develop new courses for a dance program	**Teaching:** Academic service learning **Research:** Participatory action research **Choreography and Performance:** Community-based performance **Service:** Develop and disseminate national standards for dance education
Low scholarship, low engagement	**Low scholarship, high engagement**
Teaching: One-time dance workshop for dance students **Research:** Presenting pilot data **Choreography and Performance:** Dance composition students perform solos in class **Service:** Give a one-time talk about the history of jazz dance to a high school class	**Teaching:** University students teach lessons to other members of the class **Research:** Administer exit survey after 10 weeks of afterschool dance teaching **Choreography and Performance:** Students throughout the campus perform as a flash mob to advertise the dance program **Service:** Give a series of six talks on jazz dance to a high school class

WRAP-UP

Public scholarship in dance presents both opportunities and challenges because of the complexities of moving scholarship beyond the walls of the college or university. Kolb's experiential learning model, coupled with the outreach and engagement continuum, influenced the design of the public scholarship in dance quadrant. Additional assistance in developing projects is provided by checklists that enable you to assess teaching, research, choreography, and service scholarship. While not all public scholarship in dance has to occur at the highest level of engagement and scholarship, the models and examples in this book will make the creation of deeply engaged projects an easier task.

2

TEACHING

Service learning provides college and university students with a "community context" to their education, allowing them to connect their academic course work to their roles as citizens.

Seifer and Conners, *Faculty Toolkit for Service-Learning in Higher Education*

When dance educators create opportunities for students to connect their learning with the larger community, everyone benefits. The students apply their learning and in the process gain communication, civic, and social skills. The community becomes a partner with the university in developing mutually beneficial experiences, and the faculty member benefits by expanding the network of collaborators, potential students, and audience members. *Academic service learning* is the term for this form of teaching.

Service learning differs significantly from volunteerism and internships because of the reciprocal nature of this pedagogical tool. With volunteerism, students provide a service that may or may not be connected to academic goals; in an internship, students perform tasks that are integrally connected to academic outcomes. However, the goals are not necessarily connected to service. Academic service learning is a high-impact educational practice that pushes students out of their comfort zones. Students connect and apply their learning in a real-world setting. Through written reflections (a critical component of service learning), faculty members are able to assess gains in students' skills and knowledge. For example, in an article about the impact of academic service learning in a dance and drama course, thematic analyses of the students' reflective journals written in response to a specific teaching session allowed the faculty scholar to conclude that the course promoted a deeper understanding of course content; allowed the students to develop skills in lesson planning, teaching, assessment, and reflection; enabled students to develop an understanding of interdisciplinary approaches to teaching dance and drama; and helped students relate course content to future career goals (Overby 2004).

Campus Compact, a national organization established to support service learning and other community engagement projects, provides many resources that support the development, implementation, and assessment of service learning. Their website provides information to assist with the development of relationships with community partners, strategies for preparing student and community knowledge, and reflective activities that affect student learning (2012).

Service learning is beneficial to all partners when it is carefully developed with strong community partners, clear connections with the academic content, adequate time in the community setting, and various reflection strategies. The partners in the service learning project are a faculty member, a student, and a community partner (e.g., classroom teachers, K-12 students, parents). Reflective strategies—a key component of service learning experiences—may take the form of written responses to prompts related to the experience. They may also include illustrations or artistic expressions such as a poem or choreography related to the experience.

The examples that follow exemplify the best in academic service learning. Miriam Giguere's service learning courses are described with Kolb's model of experiential learning as a guide. The examples contributed by Karen Kaufmann and Marita Cardinal provide more contextual information about the service learning experiences without the Kolb model.

LINDY SCHOLARS AND MENTORS

Instructor

Miriam Giguere

University Partner

Drexel University

Community Partner

Lindy Scholars Program (three West Philadelphia middle schools)

Description of Project

The Lindy Scholars Program promotes the integration of real-world teaching into the DANC 340: Dance Pedagogy course offered at Drexel University. Students learn both theory and practice for dance teaching. Each of the 12 to 15 students in the course creates two sample lessons, which they execute in the class with their peers, and then they teach a third lesson with the Lindy Scholars program. Lindy Scholars is a program for students in three public middle schools in West Philadelphia. Students in the program receive tutoring twice a week from Drexel students in math and reading at their home school. Students from the public schools are referred to as Lindy scholars. Students from Drexel who work with them are referred to as Lindy mentors. Every other Saturday, the Lindy scholars go to Drexel's campus for a series of enrichment activities, including dance classes taught by the students in DANC 340 under the supervision of Miriam Giguere, the course instructor.

Each of the peer lessons that the Drexel students prepare ends with students giving each other anonymous feedback on the lesson as well as receiving written information from the instructor. While the peers are writing their feedback, the student who taught the lesson (referred to as the teaching student) writes an immediate self-reflection. The written feedback from peers and instructor is shared with the teaching student, who writes a second postactivity self-reflection, which includes reflection on their feedback as well. The teaching student then meets with the instructor for a debriefing of the teaching activity and to set new goals for the next teaching experience. The students complete two peer teaching activities in class before they teach in the Lindy Scholars program. This ensures that the Lindy scholars receive the best possible student instruction. Table 2.1 presents Giguere's work in Kolb's experiential learning model.

Assessment

Assessment of the project happens on two levels. The success of the individual Drexel students participating is assessed through Giguere's observation of each student's execution of the teaching plan. The criteria for success are established with the student during two individual meetings, one after each peer teaching experience in class. The student's third teaching experience, with the Lindy scholars, is debriefed and assessed in a small-group meeting with the three or four co-teachers after the lesson. At the conclusion of each

TABLE 2.1 Teaching Academic Service Learning: Lindy Scholars and Mentors

Kolb's model	Actions	Outcomes
Phase 1 Concrete experiences	Students study educational theory and pedagogical methods for teaching in an urban school setting.	Students read about ways in which dance can be taught as a discrete subject and ways in which dance can be used as a tool for learning other subject matter.
Phase 2 Observation and reflection	Students observe and reflect.	Students go through sample lessons in class led by the instructor demonstrating methods for engagement with middle school students. Students in the course alternate participating and observing the lesson. Each demonstration ends in a written reflection.

Kolb's model	Actions	Outcomes
Phase 3 Forming abstract concepts	Students design activities based on experiences and observations.	Students create sample lessons and lesson plans for dance classes with middle school students. Students decide on the principle to teach as well as the method of teaching. They execute these plans in the class with peers. Each peer teaching session ends in anonymous written feedback from peers as well as written feedback from the teacher while the students who taught the lesson self-reflect. After receiving the feedback, the student teacher writes another reflection and meets with the faculty member to go over the session and to set goals for the next teaching experience.
Phase 4 Testing in new situations	Students actively engage in applying learning in a new environment.	After two peer teaching sessions, students select the most successful lesson to teach to the middle school Lindy scholars. Lessons are bundled, so there are three or four student teachers covering a class with Lindy scholars on each Saturday session.
Dissemination	Students create performances, lesson plans, and formal reflections.	Students create a culminating activity for the Lindy scholars and their families at the end-of-year celebration. Students lead repetitions of the most successful dance exercises from the 10-week session, culminating in an informal performance for attendees of the final-day event. Students submit teaching journals, which include all written feedback, lesson plans, and multiple self-reflections from the three teaching experiences.

school year, Giguere and the coordinator of the Lindy Scholars program, Shayla Amenra, assess the overall success of the program. Issues of Lindy Scholar engagement, length of the activities, frequency of the activities, and so on are discussed and adjusted if necessary for the following year.

WHEELCHAIR DANCE
CLASS COLLABORATION

Instructor
Miriam Giguere

University Partner
Drexel University

Community Partner
HMS School for Children with Cerebral Palsy

Description of Project
This project is a partnership between Drexel University dance program and the Home of the Merciful Savior (HMS) School for Children with Cerebral Palsy. For 60 minutes each Tuesday afternoon from October through June, dance students at Drexel partner with students from HMS School for a wheelchair dance class. Each Drexel student is assigned one HMS student for the entirety of the project. There are usually approximately 24 students involved in total, 12 from Drexel and 12 from HMS. The class, which takes place at the HMS School, is led by Rachel Federman-Morales, a dance and movement therapist on staff at HMS. All of the students from HMS who participate are in wheelchairs, and 75 percent are nonverbal. The Drexel students range in age from 17 to 22; the HMS students range in age from 14 to 21.

The class consists of a warm-up phase in which the HMS students, with assistance from their Drexel partners, attempt to increase range of motion in the arms, legs, and neck. The next phase of class explores the use of a prop such as a parachute or other tactile stimulation with which the group can interact. Finally, an idea for a dance is explored and choreography is developed. Past themes for the choreography include the ocean, colors, and works of Isadora Duncan. Because the Drexel and HMS students stay with the same partner for the duration of the project, an opportunity for true rapport and a relationship can develop. It takes a considerable commitment of time and energy for the Drexel dancers to establish communication with their HMS partners, but participating students report that this can be the most rewarding part of the process.

The project culminates in two performances. The first takes place in mid-April at the HMS School at the annual volunteer appreciation night, which is attended by the parents of the HMS students. The second performance takes place at Drexel University's Mandell Theater in early June. The HMS students perform in the Youth Performance Exchange matinee, which includes dances by students from several public schools involved in the Drexel dance program's school residency projects and dances performed by the Drexel Dance Ensemble. Table 2.2 presents the project in Kolb's experiential learning model.

TABLE 2.2 Teaching Academic Service Learning: Wheelchair Dance Class Collaboration

Kolb's model	Actions	Outcomes
Phase 1 Concrete experiences	Teacher provides many concrete examples of service learning.	Dance majors interested in pursuing careers in dance and movement therapy, physical therapy, or education are invited to participate in the project so that they can gain experience in being in a helping role and see the possibilities of developing a therapeutic relationship.
Phase 2 Observation and reflection	Students observe and reflect.	Students go with their instructor to the HMS School for Children with Cerebral Palsy on an introductory observation and orientation visit. They are given readings about cerebral palsy, are shown video of the project from previous years, and meet their potential partners who are teens in wheelchairs.
Phase 3 Forming abstract concepts	Students design activities based on their experiences and observations.	Students return to the HMS School once a week from October through June to serve as partners for the HMS students in a wheelchair dance class.
Phase 4 Testing in new situations	Students actively engage in applying learning in a new environment.	The weekly wheelchair dance class culminates in two performances, one at the HMS School for parents of the HMS participants and a second performance at Drexel University as part of the Youth Performance Exchange Matinee at the Mandell Theater. This performance involves student performers from other Philadelphia Schools where Drexel teaches dance classes, with 400 students in attendance.

(continued)

Table 2.2 *(continued)*

Kolb's model	Actions	Outcomes
Dissemination	Students express ideas through reflective essays, posters, interviews, off-campus presentations, websites, journal articles, dance, drama, visual art, or music.	Students participate in an interview with the coordinating Drexel faculty member (not the leader of the HMS class) explaining what they have learned about dance and about themselves through the HMS School wheelchair dance collaboration. The data are transcribed and charted. The information has been shared with educators at a research fair at Drexel University, the National Dance Educators Organization Conference, and the Congress on Research in Dance. Students attended these events to give their views and comments on what they learned through this process.

Assessment

The assessment of success for the participating students is based on their reflections in interviews and on the faculty observations of the students' ability to develop a cooperative relationship with their partners. The preliminary research on the effects of this project on students at Drexel is qualitative; interviews with students on their lived experiences in this project are transcribed and summarized. This data mining leads to the identification of themes and categories that categorize the experience of learning through the wheelchair dance project.

The student impact of this project is profound (figure 2.1). The dance program at Drexel focuses on preparing students for one of three graduate options: a master's degree in elementary education, a master's degree in dance and movement therapy, or a doctoral degree in physical therapy. Dance majors at Drexel complete a threshold review, which is an interview with the faculty of the graduate program they hope to enter at the end of the undergraduate portion of their education. During the last three years of threshold reviews, all of the students who participated in the wheelchair dance collaboration have described it as pivotal to their understanding of themselves and what they hope to do in their dance-related careers.

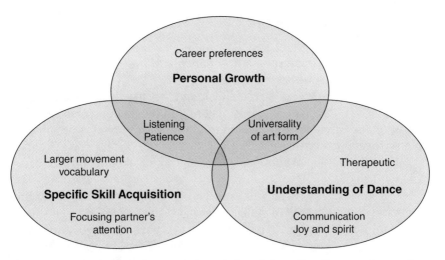

Figure 2.1 University students gain knowledge, skills, and a deeper understanding of the power of dance.

SERVICE LEARNING PROGRAMS IN DANCE EDUCATION

Instructor

Marita Cardinal

University Partner

Western Oregon University, Division of Health and Physical Education. Primary students are undergraduates majoring in early childhood or elementary education, physical education, and dance; additional students include those in undergraduate liberal arts.

Community Partner

Primary partners are local homeschooled families. Additional partners have included WOU Child Development Center, Monmouth-Independence YMCA, Luckiamute Valley Charter Schools, Falls City Elementary School, Talmadge Middle School, Independence Wagon Wheelers Square Dancers, and Salem Clare Bridge Group Home for Seniors.

Description of Project

The purpose of this project is to share the homeschool program, an example of a service learning program in dance and movement education at Western Oregon University (figure 2.2).

This profile presents a successful long-term teacher education program in which university students majoring in dance education, physical education, or elementary education teach groups of local homeschooled youth who attend classes on campus approximately once a week. Program history, organization, instructional processes, and assessment methods are described.

The homeschool program has evolved as part of a variety of teacher education courses taught in the Division of Health and Physical Education over many years. Changes in program structure have occurred as the result of curricular revisions, faculty changes, facility availability, course developments, population changes, and ongoing feedback from all parties. In the current homeschool program courses, university students learn by doing through the following practicum process of cyclical teaching:

1. Learning movement pedagogy (which includes observation of and participation in a variety of movement education lessons)
2. Researching lesson ideas
3. Planning lessons
4. Creating and gathering teaching materials
5. Teaching lessons

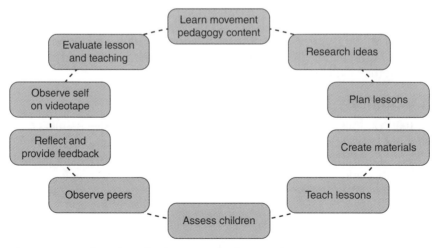

Figure 2.2 Students learn by doing: Cardinal service learning course.

6. Assessing children's performance
7. Observing peers' teaching performances
8. Reflecting on data collected and providing feedback to peers
9. Observing own teaching on video
10. Evaluating personal lesson quality and teaching effectiveness

Local homeschooling families are invited to participate in a series of movement education lessons, associated with various university courses, as they become available. Communication is primarily done by e-mail, although an Internet group site was created and used in the past. Efforts are made to involve these families in at least one series of approximately six to eight lessons every school year, and they are often invited to participate in additional courses. The teaching practicum events are held in one large gymnasium where multiple groups of children are taught simultaneously by small groups of university students. Lessons last approximately one hour, and time is divided among the student teachers, each of whom teaches 15- to 20-minute lessons. From 20 to 100 children between the ages of 2 and 13 have attended lessons on any given day. The children are grouped by age level into four to eight teaching groups. For each lesson, the college students are organized in small groups and rotate among the roles of lead teacher, assistant teacher, videographer, and observer. Each week, the college students rotate among teaching groups and among groups of children, which provides them opportunities to learn from their peers and teach all ages. The college students teach a variety of movement experiences to the children with a different theme each week, including creative dance, recreational dance, rhythmic activities with equipment, and gymnastics. Each week, the college students practice varied teaching methods and conduct different systematic observational techniques for peer feedback. All lessons are video recorded and students observe, reflect on, and evaluate their own teaching quality. Final video presentations allow students to showcase evidence of their teaching effectiveness.

Coordination of the homeschool program takes considerable time, effort, and communication. Time is spent teaching the university students not only what and how to teach in terms of movement but also how the overall practicum occurs each week and how each student must participate in and take responsibility for the facilitation of the event. Each student is therefore assigned one responsibility, task, or duty that he or she will conduct each week to ensure the teaching practicum event runs smoothly.

The students are graded on their written lesson plans, teaching presentations, student assessments, participation in the peer feedback process, self-teaching evaluations and reflections, final filmed presentation that showcases their performance of selected teaching behaviors, final written reflection, and service learning projects for the homeschooling families that extend beyond their actual lessons. Results of the qualitative survey show that college students in these courses prefer learning through hands-on teaching experiences with real children. Survey responses from parents of homeschooled children in this program are positive.

Assessment

College students' grades are based on the quality of their academic materials (lesson plans, systematic observations, reflections, and iMovie showcase of teaching behaviors). Program effectiveness of this project is evaluated through qualitative responses from college student course evaluations and homeschooling parents' surveys (see figures A.5 and A.6 in the appendix). Qualitative data from surveys are summarized, common themes are identified, and specific examples are highlighted.

TEACHING MOVEMENT IN THE SCHOOLS

Instructor

Karen Kaufmann

University Partner

University of Montana

Community Partners

Local K-12 schools

Description of Project

Service learning is celebrated and encouraged at the University of Montana. Courses that include service learning are designated as such in the course guide. Each semester faculty provide statistics to the Office of Civic Engagement about the numbers of students, number of hours spent in the communities, assessment processes, and community partners. UM's dance program has three courses designated as service learning; for the purposes of this book, experiences gained in DANC 497: Teaching Movement in the Schools are described.

DANC 497 is a requirement for BFA dance majors with a concentration in teaching, art education students, and music pedagogy students. The participants' backgrounds in various arts provide a rich environment for the class, but at first the class feels slightly biased toward the dance majors. The playing field is leveled out about eight weeks into the semester. All

Service learning student leads elementary students in an opening activity.

class materials are posted on Moodle, an online course website where students access the syllabus, readings, and assignments; submit work; and view their grades. Discussion forums are used as well.

Scholarly Content: The Basis for Service Learning

The service learning section of the class makes up one-fifth of the semester and involves three weeks of school visits. The first nine weeks of the course are structured around scholarly learning in dance education. Knowledge areas include the role movement plays in brain development, developmental movement patterns, theory of multiple intelligences, national and state standards for dance, lesson planning, and child development. Early on, students have opportunities to teach mini-lessons and a basic movement warm-up. Students learn principles of abstraction and have opportunities to develop movement prompts that go beyond pantomime and acting out ideas and delve into using the rich movement language to dance the curriculum.

An introduction to curricular integration results in assignments that use creative movement to teach content areas (science, math, social studies, language arts, music, and art). Numerous movement examples are provided each week, using creative movement to teach diverse areas of the K-12 curriculum. Students are taught about embedded assessment methodologies and the multiple ways in which a dance teacher can ascertain whether students are learning the intended objectives.

Six weeks into the semester, students take a quiz measuring their knowledge of the elements of dance, curriculum integration, dance education theory, and content. The quiz is the catalyst that jump-starts students to dig into the material and go from familiarity to mastery. Students who were mildly engaged with the course content grab hold while studying for the test. The quiz focuses on information that the students will directly need for the service learning project.

Setting Up the Service Learning Project

Early in the semester, students form pairs and select a grade level for the service learning project. As the professor, Kaufmann makes personal contacts with public and private school teachers throughout the community, inviting them to serve as host teachers. Students' requests for grade levels and subject matter are taken into account: Art education students are placed in high school art classes, music pedagogy students in elementary music classes, and dance students in elementary and middle school classrooms. Once placed, students contact host teachers to introduce themselves and set up the teaching schedule. Kaufmann provides her students with a sample introductory e-mail to ensure they set a positive, professional tone so the relationship between the college student and host teacher starts off on the right foot (figure A.7, in the appendix). An official letter is sent to each host teacher with a final evaluation form for each student and a self-addressed stamped envelope to help them easily return the form.

Curricular Integration Plan

After the quiz, students develop an individual curricular integration plan (known as the CIP)—a mini-lesson plan that serves as their first experience in selecting a curricular topic and conceiving and developing learning activities to help them teach that concept—along with one or more dance concepts. Research about the content area is required before they develop movement prompts for teaching the content.

On the day the assignment is due, students workshop the CIP in small groups, reading their movement prompts, hearing how it sounds, and seeing the movement responses of their peers. Students respond to one another's plan by providing feedback on things they appreciate about the CIP and giving "what-if" suggestions to the lessons' authors, which provide the authors with new ideas to think about. This class leads to a stimulating and rich discussion, often raising new questions and greater awareness about the art of successful curriculum integration. Students may submit their CIPs for grading, or they can take it home, revise it, and submit it the next day via e-mail for grading. Most students take advantage of the opportunity to make revisions.

Generally at this point in the semester, students express nervousness about their upcoming service learning project, raise concerns about whether they know enough to teach in the schools, and question what kinds of activities are appropriate for their intended grade levels. Students are now ready to delve deeper into the child development materials they've read now that the material is directly relevant to them.

In-Class Teaching

Next, students collaborate with their partners to develop a full, integrated lesson plan geared to the grade level they'll be teaching for their service learning projects (see figure A.8, in the appendix). They begin by selecting and researching a content area in the district curriculum and collaboratively develop a full lesson plan using dance and movement to teach the content area. Students continue the process developed previously, recognizing what they like about their own lesson plan and identifying what-ifs that could improve it. The following week, each team teaches their lesson to the class, receiving peer feedback and hearing discussion about the learning design and the teaching techniques. See the time line that follows:

First 9 Weeks

1. Scholarly content: the basis of service learning.
2. Quiz on content.
3. Students develop an individual curricular integration plan (CIP) mini-lesson.
4. Students workshop the CIP in small groups.
5. Students collaborate with partners to develop a full, integrated lesson plan.
6. Students teach lesson to class.
7. Entire class visits one school and teaches a lesson in groups of four.

Weeks 10, 11, and 12

8. Two weeks of classes are cancelled for service learning experience.
9. Pairs visit their classroom four times, teaching twice and assisting partner twice.

Weeks 13, 14, and 15

10. Students share experiences.
11. Students submit a service learning portfolio.

Two Initial School Visits

After teaching an integrated lesson plan to the class, the entire class visits a school together for a 45-minute class period. Most recently, the 16 students in DANC 497 split into groups of four and collaboratively designed and taught a lesson plan about bats in second-grade classrooms (there are four second-grade classes at this school). Teaching in groups of four was a way to ease them into the service learning project because they had three peers as support and their first experience involved only about 7 to 8 minutes of teaching. Debriefing after the class led to a lively discussion about the children's joy while moving and their creative responses to the movement prompts. It also deepened the students' interest in delving more fully into classroom management strategies, an area they revisit immediately before they go into the schools.

Immediately after the peer-supported teaching experience, students visit their service learning classroom, meet the teacher, observe the teacher's style, meet the students, see the teaching space, and get a feel for the general school environment. They write their initial observations, which serve as the first part of the service learning portfolio documenting their experiences (see figure A.9, in the appendix).

Service Learning Project: Teaching Creative Movement in K-12 Schools

Students' lives are busy. In addition to taking 15 to 21 credits, most hold part-time jobs, and many have families and are raising children. Several years ago, Kaufmann dropped the idea of asking students to find extra time to schedule their service learning project; therefore, she cancels two weeks of classes, enabling them to schedule their teaching during class time. Even though some service learning classes are scheduled at other times during the week (depending on school schedules, recess, and so on), the majority use the class period for teaching.

Pairs visit their classroom four times; each is required to teach twice and assist the partner in teaching. Beforehand, students get curricular information from the teacher, including the target learning, specific vocabulary, and worksheets or curriculum provided by the teacher. Students develop the learning activity, teach it, and assess its effectiveness. They also are required to assess each of their partner's lessons.

Assessment

Everyone finds it refreshing to leave campus and go into the schools for two weeks. When they come back together, it is with a renewed sense of accomplishment. Kaufmann notices a visible transformation in her students. Students share their experiences with the class; discuss their successes, challenges, and foibles; and describe classroom stories. They turn in a service learning portfolio with their baseline observation, detailed lesson plans, and in-depth evaluations about their own teaching and what they learned from assisting their partner teaching. An overview of the experience evaluates the scope of the learning and asks the students to define new questions that they have developed as a result of the experience.

As a university professor, Kaufmann often feels some uncertainty and nervousness immediately before sending her students out to teach. She states, "Will Laura have the confidence to manage 22 active fourth-graders?" "Will John be able to speak coherently to kindergarteners?" As a professor, it requires confidence, relinquishment of control, and trust in the bigger picture with the knowledge that the best way to prepare someone to teach is to offer a real-world experience for the student to just do it. "In the end, I'm never disappointed and am confident that this university-based service learning course will serve as the foundation to be built upon and developed throughout their teaching careers."

WRAP-UP

The examples in this chapter provide clear models for the development of future service learning courses. Service learning courses should include guided self-reflection, peer teaching before in-school teaching, background information about the developmental needs of students, appropriate content and pedagogy skills, authentic assessments, and a reciprocal relationship with the community partner. See figure 2.3 for the public scholarship in dance quadrant.

Academic service learning courses expand the reach of dance for many community members. The dance faculty members who contributed the examples in this chapter spent additional time collaborating

FIGURE 2.3   PUBLIC SCHOLARSHIP IN DANCE QUADRANT FOR TEACHING

High scholarship, low engagement	High scholarship, high engagement
	Giguere Cardinal Kaufmann
Low scholarship, low engagement	Low scholarship, high engagement

with teachers in the community and preparing students to teach in the community. However, all partners benefitted—the students gained pedagogy skills and knowledge, the faculty members gained access to teachers and students in the community, and the community partners gained experience in dance education. Together, the dance faculty, students, and community partners gained unique experiences that could not have happened if the dance faculty had remained on their campuses.

3

CHOREOGRAPHY

The way that choreographers organize minds, bodies, ideas, money, institutions and people, and their own lives untangles a natural process for practical use. Because we are very practical. We are also funny, sad, hard, hard-working, and very independent. We resemble cowboys and wrestlers in our feistiness, seamstresses in our ability to piece together unity and connection when it is needed.

Liz Lerman, *Hiking the Horizontal*

Choreography and the choreographic process are unique to dance. Unlike the previous discussion about teaching or the future chapters on research and service, choreography falls directly into the realm of dance. As a creative process, choreography may be separated into stages similar to the scientific process. The choreographer begins with an image or idea; through exploration, revision, and abstraction, the choreographer applies elements of form to produce a final product. The choreographers highlighted in this chapter provide insight into a choreographic process that has been directly connected to the larger community. The results of these efforts have expanded the reach of this artistic process for the benefit of dance teachers and the community partners.

In the choreography examples that follow, Kolb's model provides a structure that allows you to visualize the planning, implementation, and assessment of the community-engaged choreographic process. In the Gingrasso example, the model is applied from the perspective of the dancers. In the examples from Magruder, Corbin, and Overby, the model is applied from the perspective of the choreographer. In both applications the phases of concrete experiences, observation and reflection, forming abstract concepts, and testing in a new situation are included.

The choreography highlighted in this chapter involves a range of community partners and locations, including adults in the community, arts councils and schools, and a prairie preserve. Moreover, the impact is felt locally and nationally. All of the projects push the boundaries of dance beyond the walls of the university.

CHOREOGRAPHING ORAL HISTORIES: MINING SOCIAL AND CULTURAL ISSUES IN YOUR COMMUNITY THROUGH CONCERT DANCE

Type of Project
Choreography

Choreographer
Susan Gingrasso

University Partner
University of Wisconsin at Stevens Point theatre and dance department

Community Partners

Community members in Stevens Point

Description of Project

Gingrasso created three choreographic works based on the oral histories of three Stevens Point populations: women (*Across the Paths We Have Made*, 2000), men (*everybody has a story*, 2003), and those who have been dropped from the workforce (*Dropped: Picking Up the Pieces*, 2004). The works occurred from 2000 to 2004. Each project took approximately 10 months from inception to performance.

The process included collecting oral histories from community members and transcribing the interviews, which led to improvisations and the final choreography and performances. During the performances, the community members (as audience members) gave feedback to the cast, enabling the choreography to become more expressive and real.

For the first two pieces, *Across the Paths We Have Made* and *everybody has a story*, Gingrasso engaged the community participants in movement improvisation sessions because she wanted to let their ideas drive the overall direction of each piece. Each 1.5-hour session revolved around ideas generated by the group that became the themes for individual and group improvisations. These movement sessions brought Gingrasso closer to the participants and helped her craft the form and direction for each piece. For *Dropped: Picking Up the Pieces*, the geographic distance of those who agreed to participate precluded her ability to work with the seven participants in movement sessions.

For the women's and men's oral history pieces, interview questions emerged from ideas generated in the movement sessions. For the work *Dropped: Picking Up the Pieces*, research about job loss, identity, and finding a new career direction generated interview questions. The questions were provided to each participant well in advance of the interview.

In selecting specific vignettes from each interview, each vignette had to

- convey a complete story or idea,
- contribute integrally to the overall structure,
- require little digital editing,
- revolve around an idea that could be explored choreographically, and
- communicate energy through vocal effort.

The edited vignettes became the script as well as the sound score for each piece.

Creating a script from participant interviews took hours of culling ideas from the transcribed interviews, selecting the appropriate vignettes from the recorded interviews, digitally editing the vignettes, and finding an order for the vignettes to provide the work with the right shape. The vignettes varied greatly in length. The shortest was 6 seconds, the longest 3 minutes. Each work used 20 to 25 vignettes and ranged from 25 to 35 minutes in length (see figure 3.1).

The members of each cast developed a phenomenal community among themselves and formed strong bonds with interviewees. Through working with real-life stories, the young adult performers from the university learned valuable life lessons. They approached the development of material with honesty and integrity because they felt a responsibility to the community members whose lives they represented in movement.

Interviewees attended rehearsals and provided essential feedback to cast members and to Gingrasso from their perspective. Cast members asked questions about the events in specific vignettes. Community participants saw cast members bringing their stories to life in movement, which gave their own stories new relevance.

The participants in the oral history project brought their friends and friends of friends into the theater; most of these people had never seen a dance concert. They filled the theater. Many attended several performances because they were deeply touched by life stories that could easily be theirs.

These works, so connected to their community—their stories and their voices—drew a new audience for dance into the theater. Gingrasso and cast members presented these works, by invitation, at two national Small Cities Conferences and the Sociologists of Minnesota and Wisconsin Sociological Association.

John Strassburg, accompanist for the UWSP dance program, composed the music, a textural musical score. The music lies over the voices for each piece.

ACROSS THE PATHS WE HAVE MADE

(A suite of vignettes in five scenes)
    Prologue
    Scene I: Remembering Childhood
    Scene II: In and Out of Relationships
    Scene III: Being a Parent
    Scene IV: Conflict and Convergence
    Scene V: Across Our Paths

Figure 3.1 A listing of the vignettes created for the choreography in Gingrasso's *Across the Paths We Have Made.*

Assessment

Since this is an arts-based research project, one of the assessments includes the embodied stories brought to life for both the performers and audience members. Success is determined by the existence and meaningfulness of these stories that did not exist before the performance. Table 3.1 presents Gingrasso's work in Kolb's experiential learning model.

TABLE 3.1   Public Scholarship in Choreography: Choreographing Oral Histories

Kolb's model	Actions	Outcomes
Phase 1 Concrete experiences	Cast members listen to stories of community members.	Cast members develop stories into short vignettes.
Phase 2 Observation and reflection	Cast members observe and reflect on each group's choreography.	Cast members create movement based on the vignettes. They share choreography, give and receive feedback, and revise choreography.
Phase 3 Forming abstract concepts	Cast members abstract words into movement metaphors.	Cast members select key words in vignettes to abstract into movement metaphors.
Phase 4 Testing in new situations	Cast members perform in multiple venues.	Cast members stage and organize the vignettes for performances in several venues.
Dissemination	Cast members perform and make scholarly presentations.	Performances: • UWSP Faculty Dance Concert • Two libraries in Wisconsin Conference presentations: • Small Cities and Smart Growth Conference at UWSP 2000 • Sociological Association Conference 2003 • National Dance Education Conference 2004

MAGRUDER PROJECT 1: DANCE IN THE SCHOOLS

Project Type
Choreography and performance

Choreographers
Ella and Mark Magruder

University Partner
Ripon College

Community Partners
Green Giant Corporation and Wisconsin Arts Board

Description of Project
Mark and Ella Magruder choreographed and performed duets for grades 1, 3, 5, 7, and 8 in the local public schools and then taught a series of one-week creative dance lessons in each grade level and in every classroom for all the students who had seen the performance. Funded entirely by a corporate grant and a smaller state arts board grant, the project lasted for two years. They taught in several schools during the two years. In each school they also provided five creative dance lessons for each grade. This could take up to two months per school. The format included 15 minutes of audience participation at the end of the performance to help the children invest in the project before their classroom experience. The choreography included *Cloud Shadow* (a piece inspired by a nature study of shadowed landscapes), *Hurricane's Coming* (a kinetic work with spins and explosive bursts of energy), *Timeago* (a duet based on early human society that became a Magruder signature work), and *To the Jitters* (a frenetic dance about anxiety and fast-paced life). Table 3.2 presents the Magruders' work in Kolb's experiential learning model.

Assessment
All students complete formal pre- and postperformance assessment checklists and surveys. A preperformance survey found that boys did not want to see the performance but the girls did. On a postperformance survey, boys enjoyed the performance and wanted to see it again. Girls continued to express enjoyment of the performance.

TABLE 3.2   Public Scholarship in Choreography: Dance in the Schools

Kolb's model	Actions	Outcomes
Phase 1 Concrete experiences	Cast members research topics of educational relevance.	Cast members select specific topics to develop into choreography.
Phase 2 Observation and reflection	Cast members begin improvising and revising choreography. They partner with a psychologist.	Cast members develop choreographic motifs. They plan to collect performance and teaching data for before-and-after effects.
Phase 3 Forming abstract concepts	Using movement metaphors, cast members continue designing choreography.	Cast members make a performance of original choreography focused on the needs and interests of school-age students.
Phase 4 Testing in new situations	Cast members finalize choreographic production. They use data to enhance performing, teaching effectiveness, and mentoring.	Cast members perform, teach classes in local schools, or become artists in residence. The experience guides college students to new avenues and careers.
Dissemination	Students publish data.	Students write about the project for publication in a professional journal.

MAGRUDER PROJECT 2: PERFORMING IN NATIONAL VENUES

Project Type

Choreography and performance

Choreographers

Ella and Mark Magruder

University Partner

University of Montana

Community Partners

Bargemusic in New York City, MoMing in Chicago, The Dance Place in Washington, DC

Description of Project

The Magruders performed solos and duets in Chicago, New York City, and Washington, DC. The dances are set to three original scores by composer Paul Seitz. *Things That Wash Up* is based on a poem of the same name from the Swampy Cree, a Canadian indigenous tribe, which explores how two individuals face adversity together and separately. *Stones* is a solo about human rights violations of women and death by stoning. *River Dance* is a flowing abstract work with a score sung by soprano Christine Seitz and set to a poem about the East River in New York City. The tour also included *Lonesome Heart of the Prairie* (a comic solo about a would-be cowboy who has marital woes), *Rags for Eurreal* (a comic duet to ragtime music by Eurreal Montgomery where the gag is that the dancers change their costumes on stage), and *Thanatos* (from the Greek word for death, a duet portraying death as a gentle, seductive stalker and set to music of a Japanese bamboo flute). Table 3.3 presents the Magruders' work in Kolb's experiential learning model.

TABLE 3.3 Public Scholarship in Choreography: Performance in National Venues

Kolb's model	Actions	Outcomes
Phase 1 Concrete experiences	Choreographers research topics of interest and select potential artistic partners.	Choreographers focus on topics of interest to a primarily adult population of audience members; topics are selected for their educational and entertainment value.
Phase 2 Observation and reflection	Choreographers collaborate with artistic partners and choreograph, revise, and rework dances.	Choreographers set up first (test run) performance at the university before the tour. They bring in choreographer and performer Beverly Blossom. As mentor, she has good suggestions and apt criticisms for the Magruders' duets and then performs with them.

Kolb's model	Actions	Outcomes
Phase 3 Forming abstract concepts	They finalize choreography.	They prepare to share the interarts choreographic project.
Phase 4 Testing in new situations	They present choreography.	They present choreography in main venues in NYC, Chicago, and DC.
Dissemination	Choreographers compile reviews and media to serve as evidence of excellence of artistic merit (research and scholarship).	Choreographers provide evidence of national recognition to the university in the form of updates to curriculum vitae.

Assessment

Reviews of the performance by professional critiques and evidence of national recognition are provided to the university or college in the form of updates to curriculum vitae.

MAGRUDER PROJECT 3: MENAGERIE DANCE TOURING COMPANY

Type of Project
Choreography

Choreography and Professional
Nonprofit dance company

Choreographers
Ella and Mark Magruder

University Partner
Sweet Briar College is a partner only in an unofficial capacity. It allowed flexibility in academic course scheduling and provided development grants

to support the Magruders' national and international travel for conference presentation of workshops and papers for the National Dance Education Organization (NDEO) and Dance and the Child International (daCi).

Community Partner

Virginia Commission for the Arts and many local arts councils and community sponsors in Virginia and the Mid-Atlantic states

Photo courtesy of Mary Gearhart.

Mark and Ella, the Menagerie dancers performing *Environs*. Choreographed by Mark Magruder and performed by Mark and Ella Magruder, this piece premiered in Virginia in 1988. This piece is a sculptural dance in which dancers move in tubes of fabric.

Description of Project

Mark and Ella Magruder incorporated Menagerie Dance Company as a nonprofit duet company in 1984. For the next 15 years they performed for more than 100,000 young people and adults in schools, theaters, and community centers throughout the Mid-Atlantic region. The choreographers had ideas that would enhance curriculum educational goals for young audiences as well as entertain the general public. They performed original works based on these themes:

- Science: *Symbiosis* (a signature work); *Environs, Evos, Metamorphosis*
- History: *Antique Memories* (renaissance), *Jesters* (commedia dell'arte)
- Folk tales: *Peacock Maiden* (Chinese), *Flute Song* (Sioux), *Rosemary* (Italian), *Jack and the King's Girl* (Appalachian), *Fog Woman and Raven* (northwest coast)
- Abstract but concrete ideas: *Stars and Constellations* (a full-length work about the night

sky), *Cranes* (endangered birds), *Hawk's Wing* (flight), *Signs and Signals* (nonverbal signals and communication), and *Bamboo* (geometric patterns with bamboo props)

A major part of the touring was composed of workshops and lecture demonstrations in K-5 classrooms and teacher in-service workshops. Table 3.4 presents the Magruders' work in Kolb's experiential learning model.

TABLE 3.4   Public Scholarship in Choreography: Menagerie Dance Touring Company

Kolb's model	Actions	Outcomes
Phase 1 Concrete experiences	Choreographers research educational topics.	Choreographers research topics of interest to school-age population, specifically students in underserved communities.
Phase 2 Observation and reflection	They begin process of creating choreographic projects.	They choreograph, revise, and rework dances.
Phase 3 Forming abstract concepts	Choreographers finalize production.	They finalize choreography of original performances, including script writing and costume construction. Choreographers book season and perform, teach master classes and in-service workshops.
Phase 4 Testing in new situations	Choreographers perform and assess productions. They collect evaluations, comments, reviews, press.	Company performs for more than 100,000 community partners over a 15-year period. Choreographers compile and analyze experience and seek to understand reasons for successes and failures.
Dissemination	Choreographers share strategies with university students. Students apply this knowledge in their teaching and choreography and career planning.	They sponsor outreach for students through service learning experiences through lecture demonstrations and performances and master classes. They do student teaching in schools and administer and direct students in community outreach that involves teaching creative dance and choreography. They teach students how to create, market, and find funding sources for dance.

In their book *Dancing for Young Audiences* (Magruder 2013), Ella provides detailed information on creating, managing, and marketing a successful performance company. Here is their mission statement:

> *Menagerie Dance Company is a duet dance company which involves the audience so that they see, hear and feel the joy and artistry of dance and motion. . . . In each school performance, the audience sees 30 minutes of original dance followed by 15 minutes of creative audience participation where children gain first-hand knowledge of basic movement skills and creative problem solving through motion. Menagerie also offers residencies that include both performances and workshops. (p. 46)*

Assessment

Teacher assessment: Teachers completed a postperformance survey with open-ended questions. This form of assessment gave the teacher an opportunity to provide insight into the impact of this informal learning on student knowledge. The written assessment also informed the performers and choreographers about what worked and what could be improved.

ECOLOGY

Type of Project

Choreography and performance

Choreographer

Josie Metal-Corbin

University Partner

University of Nebraska at Omaha (UNO) School of HPER, music department, Writer's Workshop, biology department, and the Moving Company

Community Partners

Kaneko: Open Space for Your Mind Art Center, Green Omaha Coalition, Allwine Prairie Preserve

Description of Project

Collaboration among several departments at UNO and environmental and arts agencies in Omaha resulted in a panel presentation and a site-specific choreography for the 2010 United Nations World Environment Day in Omaha and in a performance of that work that was integrated into a cere-

Photos courtesy of David F. Conway, photographer.

Josie Metal-Corbin's work *Ecology* was part of a ceremony that dedicated prairie land to the University of Nebraska at Omaha.

mony for the dedication of prairie land to the university. See table 3.5 for details on the project in the context of Kolb's experiential learning model.

Assessment

Assessment was completed as part of an annual report describing faculty workload. This work was given a positive assessment by the university's School of Health, Physical Education and Recreation committee for annual merit review and was selected as a representation of community engagement and featured in the College of Education and UNO alumni magazines. In addition, a photo of the dance was incorporated into the college's logo as a representation of scholarly work and creative activity.

TABLE 3.5   Public Scholarship in Choreography: _Ecology_

Kolb's model	Actions	Outcomes
Phase 1 Concrete experiences	Environmentalist envisions dance integrated into a panel on the arts and the environment. Choreographer reflects on previous site-specific work.	Choreographer contacts a poet, flutist, and videographer to collaborate on a new work and selects modern dancers from university company.
Phase 2 Observation and reflection	Short studies using the poem _Ecology_ are created and experimental sessions are held with poet and musician.	Choreographer corresponds with other panelists (sculptor, glass artist, architect) to discuss scope of panel and time and space considerations.
Phase 3 Forming abstract concepts	Dance designs are filmed, assessed, and revised.	Venue coordinator consults to accommodate dancers and videographer.
Phase 4 Testing in new situations	Work is completed and viewed as part of a panel presentation.	• Panel presentation is delivered at arts center. Audience views and discusses choreography. • All collaborators and dancers visit site and confer with field manager of prairie. • Decisions are made regarding site selection for performing on the prairie grass and technical needs for poet, flutist, and videographer. • Dancers are educated in ways to protect the environment. Dance is reset on the earth and video-recorded for review. • Videographer films _Ecology_. • Dance is invited to be integrated into the inauguration of dedicated prairie land for the biology department. • Dancers perform _Ecology_.
Dissemination	Collaborators share project with larger university and alumni community.	_Ecology_ is selected as a representation of community engagement and featured in the College of Education and UNO alumni magazines. A photo of the dance is incorporated into the college's logo as a representation of scholarly work and creative activity.

KINETIC ENERGY TOURING COMPANY

Type of Project
Choreography

Choreography and Performance
Touring company

Choreographer
Lynnette Young Overby

University Partner
Michigan State University department of theatre

Community Partners
Elementary schools throughout the state of Michigan

Description of Project
The first presentation, titled *Kinetic Energy*, focuses on the concepts of kinetic and potential energy, gravity, inertia, and friction. The program is based on the Michigan Science Standards and Objectives for elementary school students: motion of objects. This standard requires all students to be able to describe and explain how and why things move as they do, demonstrate and explain how humans control the motion of objects, and relate motion to energy and energy conversions. The performance group was sponsored by the department of theatre. Brochures describing the production were mailed to elementary schools throughout Michigan. Each school paid a small fee for the 45-minute production. The funds were used for costumes, the portable set, and stipends for the performers. The first *Kinetic Energy* program took the form of a story, in which a science student returns to his old elementary school to teach the children about physical science. But before she can begin, an alien from another planet crashes in the hallway of the school. The alien needs to understand the language of motion so that he can take this knowledge back to his planet. So, with help from the students and with the physical science concepts demonstrated by the streaks of energy (university student performers), the alien is able to learn the language of motion. The program opened with the chant "Motion of Objects Groove" (figure 3.2), which introduced students to the concepts included in the presentation. At the conclusion of the program, a human spaceship is constructed by the elementary school children to blast the alien into space. Table 3.6 presents details on the project in the context of Kolb's experiential learning model.

MOTIONS OF OBJECTS GROOVE

. . . the motions of objects are easy to remember,
you use them each month from January to December
because learning is for anyone that wants to be a big star
and science is very important and it will take you very far
. . . why and what makes things move? because I like to dance and I like
to groove.
when I shake, wiggle, jump and shout,
the motions of objects are what it is all about.
. . . gravity, gravity . . . brings objects to the ground
direction, direction . . . is the actual path you are in to get around.
you go north, south, east, west, left & right,
up, down and diagonally, now you're out of sight!!
. . . the speed that we travel at is how fast that we can move,
put speed and direction together and you have
the motions of objects groove.
. . . the motions of objects groove, the motions of objects groove,
the motions of objects groove, the motions of objects groove
. . . gravity, gravity . . . brings objects to the ground
direction, direction . . . is the actual path you are in to get around.
you go north, south, east, west, left & right,
up, down and diagonally, now you're out of sight!!
. . . the speed that we travel at is how fast that we can move,
put speed and direction together and you have
the motions of objects groove.

Figure 3.2 "Motions of Objects Groove," a poem by Paulina Zionts.

TABLE 3.6 Public Scholarship in Choreography: Kinetic Energy Touring Company

Kolb's model	Actions	Outcomes
Phase 1 Concrete experiences	Choreographer contacts Michigan Department of Education to discuss potential collaboration with the development of an arts-integrated touring company.	Choreographer begins process of gaining knowledge about a specific topic based on content taught in the elementary school classrooms (e.g., force, water, light, and sound; living things).

Kolb's model	Actions	Outcomes
Phase 2 Observation and reflection	Choreography and scripts are developed; dancers and actors are selected. Collaborations with set designer and costume designer occur.	With an outline of the various scenes, choreographer and performers begin creating, observing, reflecting, and revising the scenes.
Phase 3 Forming abstract concepts	Choreography and script are finalized; set and costumes are designed. Materials are developed for distribution to schools.	Schools schedule touring company; teachers distribute preperformance materials to students.
Phase 4 Testing in new situations	University students perform for school-aged students throughout the state.	School-aged students experience an arts-integrated program that is educational and entertaining.
Dissemination	Data collected on numbers of students, schools and students impacted by performance. Choreographer and university students give local and national presentations. Program is video-recorded and educational materials are placed on a website: www.teacharts.msu.edu/pila. Presentations and publications occur.	Over 7 years of the program, more than 20,000 students and 50 teachers experience the program. Students and teachers experience an arts-integrated production that expands their knowledge of a specific area of the curriculum. They also gain appreciation of the power of the arts to educate. Overby (2000). Overby, Post, and Newman (2005).

The Kinetic Energy touring company took an arts-based approach to learning. The 45-minute productions integrated the Michigan educational standards for a specific curricular area with dance and drama. Although the program was shared with students in grades K through 5, the target for the content was fourth- and fifth-graders. Through choreography and skits, the curricular content was transformed into entertaining, educational, and accessible knowledge for K-5 students. The programs included *Kinetic Energy*, a dance and drama production based on motion of objects; *Water Works: Tales of the Hydrosphere*, based on many aspects of water; *Spark and Pop: The Adventures of Light and Sound*, based on light and sound content; and *The Kaleidoscope of Life*, based on living things including biomes and pollution. The tours took place from 1999 to 2007.

Assessment

Assessments varied with each project; however, all included a postperformance evaluation by the classroom teachers and principal. Other assessments included a survey of fourth- and fifth-grade students (the target group for the presentations) to determine the program's impact on their knowledge of scientific concepts. Students were also given the opportunity to write or draw pictures about their favorite part of the performances.

Evaluations confirmed that students gained knowledge of the specific science concepts introduced through this theatrical method. Information about the impact of this program was also submitted each year to the associate provost for engagement. The data included numbers of students, schools, and teachers and numbers of presentations and publications. Feedback from the associate provost was positive and encouraging.

WRAP-UP

Through choreography, dance educators in higher education settings can share the artistic process with multiple groups. Outcomes include a deeper personal identity, a richer understanding of place, and an educational and entertaining experience. Unlike most dance experiences, there is no age restriction when choreography is extended to community partners. Once again, all partners benefit: the university faculty member, the community at large, and the university. Figure 3.3 applies the criteria from the public scholarship in dance quadrant to the choreography quadrant.

FIGURE 3.3 PUBLIC SCHOLARSHIP IN DANCE QUADRANT FOR CHOREOGRAPHY

High scholarship, low engagement	High scholarship, high engagement
Magruder (2)	Gingrasso
Magruder (3)	Metal-Corbin
Overby	Magruder (1)
Low scholarship, low engagement	**Low scholarship, high engagement**

4

RESEARCH

. . . a partnership of students, faculty, and community members who collaboratively engage in research with the purpose of solving a pressing community problem or effecting social change.

Strand et al., *Community-Based Research and Higher Education*

When research is discussed, PhD candidates, faculty, and administrators in higher education are very clear about this term. Students who have completed PhD programs are mentored in all aspects of the research process, including developing good questions, implementing rigorous research designs, and analyzing data. The students also gain skills in professional presentations and in publishing. After graduation, the scholars begin their careers with a clear sense of progression: They must conduct research worthy of external funding—research that is destined to appear in tier 1 disciplinary journals. But research can be so much more when dance educators extend their work into their communities. Community members become partners in the research process from the formulation of the questions to the dissemination of the results. Several methodologies lend themselves to research of public scholars, including various forms of participatory action research, program evaluation, and arts-based research. Traditional experimental methods with the addition of qualitative information can also serve as an appropriate methodology.

The examples that follow model public scholarship in dance with a focus on research. Once again, Kolb's model of experiential learning is applied. The theory allows for viewing the research process and the reflective practice that promotes critical thinking and decision making.

THE MIND IN MOTION

Type of Project
Community-based research (qualitative)

Researcher
Miriam Giguere

University Partner
Drexel University

Community Partner
New Eagle Elementary School

Description of Project
This project is phase 2 of an ongoing research project into cognition during the creative process in dance. Data on children's creative process are gathered during an artist in residence project at a local elementary school. The artist in residence project involves an opening assembly for the entire

Photo courtesy of Miriam Giguere.

The Mind in Motion core group choreographing a dance about plant growth.

school followed by dance classes during the weekly physical education sessions for all students in the school. The researcher as a teaching artist teaches these. Another group, self-selected from the fifth grade and known as the core group of the residency, attends an additional daily class with the researcher or teaching artist. During this class, the core group choreographs dances in small groups to be performed at a school assembly, which concludes the residency. Core group interviews or observation data on the creative process are gathered and analyzed for the purpose of illuminating the phenomenon of cognition during the choreographic process.

Undergraduate students are involved in the residency project as performers in the opening assembly, as assistant teachers during the two-week residency, and as research assistants in transcribing data in the postresidency research analysis phase.

Assessment

This is the research question for the Mind in Motion project: What is the nature of children's thinking during the creative process in dance?

Here are research subquestions:

- What specific skills or thinking strategies can be identified from the children's process of creating dances?
- Are there specific skills that are used as the result of the collaborative nature of the project?
- Do these thinking skills or strategies appear elsewhere in the literature on cognitive or educational psychology?

The core group of students are video-recorded during their choreographic sessions. These video recordings are then transcribed with the use of descriptions of each movement and recordings of the children's verbalizations during the process. Additionally, the children are interviewed at the conclusion of the residency and asked general questions about their choreographic and aesthetic process of creating dances. These interviews are transcribed. Students also write in choreographic journals at the conclusion of each daily core group session, often answering a prompt given by the researcher asking them to recall their process in selecting and designing the movements for their dances. All three of these data sources are analyzed using a phenomenographic methodology, a research tradition that answers questions about thinking and learning (Martin 1986). Students' understanding of technical concepts is most meaningful if you look to understand their interactions with these issues from their perspective (Reed 2006). This involves close textual analysis of the transcripts, looking for themes and categories that describe the phenomenon of thinking and reasoning during these children's attempts to make meaning in movement. Three recursions of the analysis are performed until a distilled picture of cognitive process during dance creation for these children emerges. Table 4.1 presents Giguere's work in Kolb's experiential learning model.

TABLE 4.1 Public Scholarship in Dance Research: The Mind in Motion

Kolb's model	Actions	Outcomes
Phase 1 Concrete experiences	Students meet with community partner to discuss needs and read current literature.	Students are oriented to the artist in residence program and to the associated research project.
Phase 2 Observation and reflection	Students apply knowledge in the development of the project.	Students are involved in the development and performance of an opening assembly program for the artist in residence program.

Kolb's model	Actions	Outcomes
Phase 3 Forming abstract concepts	Collaboration continues to develop based on information from literature, community, and faculty.	Students act as assistant teachers to the researcher or artist in residence.
Phase 4 Testing in new situations	Students conduct research, collect data, and focus on qualitative and quantitative outcomes.	Students are actively involved in data transcription and analysis. Selected students are trained to describe what appears on the videos and transcribe audio from interviews.
Dissemination	Students produce reflective essays, posters, interviews, off-campus presentations, websites, journal articles, dance, drama, visual art, or music expressions.	Students participate in poster sessions during university-wide research day and other presentation opportunities to share what they have learned through the research process.

INTERDISCIPLINARY LEARNING THROUGH THE ARTS

Type of Project

Community-based research

Researchers

Lynnette Young Overby and ArtsBridge Scholars

Community Partners

K-12 schools

Description of Project

ArtsBridge Scholars are a group of undergraduate students who are trained to create, implement, and assess arts integration projects in local K-12 schools. The program is a part of the Office of Undergraduate Research and Experiential Learning. The other programs include the Undergraduate Research Program, the Office of Service Learning, and the McNair Scholars

Program. Each of these programs involves a 10-week summer session in addition to opportunities during the academic year. Many students in these programs continue to work in labs, schools, and community settings for two years and then complete a senior thesis during their senior year. The ArtsBridge Scholars develop lessons and assessments within their individual projects during the summer. Arts integration (an approach to teaching in which students construct and demonstrate understanding through an art form and engage in a creative process that connects an art form and another subject area, meeting evolving objectives in both; Silverstein and Layne 2010) is at the center of project development in the ArtsBridge program, making scholars advocates of high-quality arts education. See appendix A.10. The research question explored by the ArtsBridge Scholars is this: What is the effect of an arts-integrated curriculum on the cognitive, affective, and artistic knowledge of pre-K to grade 12 students?

During the academic year, the scholars collaborate with a classroom teacher. The project is then incorporated into the classroom. The lessons are modified to fit the needs of the participating students. Each project incorporates one or more art forms, including dance, music, drama, and visual art, in the teaching and assessment of academic subjects. Scholars approach the work as a research project, one in which they collect data to answer the persistent research question of the impact of arts-integrated learning on the creativity, academic achievement, and arts learning of student participants. Examples of projects are Creating Landscapes, teaching integrated dance and geography to fifth-grade students; Math That Moves You, teaching integrated music and math to third-grade students (see figure 4.1 for a sample from this project); Living History, teaching integrated dance and colonial history to fifth-grade students; and Leaps for Learning, teaching integrated dance and literacy to preschool students (see appendix A.11; the rubric was developed by ArtsBridge Scholar Julie Luzier as an assessment for students who participated in her Leaps for Learning project).

1.) Draw 3 symmetrical shapes.

Figure 4.1   Second-grade dance and math integrated project by ArtsBridge Scholar Jennifer Ryan.

Reprinted, by permission, from J. Ryan, *Math that Moves You.*

Assessment

A quasi-experimental design is used for each of the projects. A school with at least two same-grade classes is selected. The scholars create standards-based lessons including pre- and posttests of the curricular and dance content. The pretest is administered to the experimental and the control classes. The series of lessons is delivered to the experimental group. At the end of the semester, both groups are posttested. In addition to the pre- and posttests, the scholars have the students in the experimental group complete journal entries that provide qualitative information about the curricular content, dance, and other information. The University of Delaware ArtsBridge Scholars projects have produced results that support the notion that the arts have a positive impact on learning. Table 4.2 presents Overby's work in Kolb's experiential learning model.

TABLE 4.2 Public Scholarship in Dance Research: ArtsBridge Scholars of University of Delaware

Kolb's model	Actions	Outcomes
Phase 1 Concrete experiences	Students meet with community partner to discuss needs and read current literature.	Students are introduced to standards and benchmarks in specific curricular areas. They also review current research and literature in the area of interdisciplinary learning through the arts. Students are involved in writing lessons and assessments.
Phase 2 Observation and reflection	Students apply knowledge in the development of the project.	ArtsBridge Scholars observe class and reflect on teaching skills; school-age students complete journal entries after each class.
Phase 3 Forming abstract concepts	Collaboration continues to develop based on information from literature, community, and faculty.	Students are actively teaching and assessing interdisciplinary lessons. They also give pre- and posttests to the experimental and control groups. Both ArtsBridge Scholars and school-age students continue to reflect in various forms.
Phase 4 Testing in new situations	Students conduct research, collect data, and focus on qualitative and quantitative outcomes. They apply results in a new situation.	Based on collected and analyzed data, the ArtsBridge Scholars develop additional lessons and teach in a new situation.

(continued)

Table 4.2 *(continued)*

Kolb's model	Actions	Outcomes
Dissemination	Students produce reflective essays, posters, interviews, off-campus presentations, websites, journal articles, dance, drama, visual art, or music expressions.	Students participate in poster sessions during university-wide research day and other presentation opportunities to share what they have learned through the research process. The scholars have presented their research at the following conferences: • National Dance Education Organization, 2008, 2009, 2010, 2011, 2012; Dance and the Child International, Article (2013) • Formative and Summative Assessments for Dance Inter-Arts/Interdisciplinary Projects

DANCERS CONNECT

Type of Project

Case study and action research

Researchers

Mila Parrish and Emily Enloe, Dancers Connect coordinator and graduate mentor

University Partner

University of South Carolina department of theatre and dance and 20 USC dance education majors

Community Partners

Richland One School District and Richland Two School District, Columbia, South Carolina

Description of Project

Dancers Connect (DC) is a community service program at the University of South Carolina. The function of DC is twofold. First, DC is a community program in which middle school students receive high-quality instruction in ballet, modern, jazz, and hip-hop dance styles and create choreography and perform dances on the USC campus at no cost. Second, DC is a laboratory classroom and practicum teaching opportunity for preservice dance education students at USC. DC classes meet on Saturday for 2.5 hours and give interested middle school dancers the opportunity to extend their training and expertise in dance at no cost to their families. Since the initiation of the program in 2012, the DC program has served 45 community students and 20 USC preservice dance education majors and has contributed to the Columbia community.

The DC program supports dance education students by presenting an opportunity for each student to donate time and talents to the community and transform their own teaching and learning experience at USC. The DC partnership allows all participants to learn from one another by breaking down walls of exclusivity so often found in dance training. This program functions as a creative arts laboratory where all members take risks and learn from one another.

The DC program is aligned with USC service and research initiatives and is integrated in the K-12 professional teacher training program. DC program curricula support 21st-century learning skills of communication, collaboration, and creative thinking; state and national dance standards; student collaboration and expression; culturally responsive curricula; and the celebration of dance for all in the community. As a result, the undergraduate

Photo courtesy of Dr. Mila Parrish, Director of UNCG Dancers Connect.

University of South Carolina dance education student Starr Gilmer and her USC Dancers Connect students collaborate on their design dance project.

dance education students are encouraged to try out alternative pedagogical strategies that would not be possible in traditional practicum experiences because of inadequate time, inadequate space, or the number of students. By investigating alternative pedagogy and engaging in a student-centered curriculum in a supportive community, university students have begun to redefine and reframe their beliefs and values in dance education.

DC middle school students have begun to realize a more comprehensive dance curriculum, one that focuses not only on dance technique but also on aesthetic development, creative process, collaboration, and reflection. Young DC members describe being valued and knowing that participation in the program not only educates them but also supports the training of future dance educators. Such innovations in pedagogical practice not only influence dance instruction now but also may influence the way that dance is taught in years to come.

Project Goals

Following are the goals for the Dancers Connect community partnership:

- Provide free high-quality dance instruction for community students, which is aligned with state and national dance standards.
- Build a creative community supporting the needs of all learners in celebration of dance as a creative and expressive art form.
- Assist every student, regardless of race, ethnicity, income, geographical location, or disability, in learning, creating, and sharing dance.
- Broaden students' perspectives and afford them a new way to think, perceive, and imagine.
- Support the practicum needs of USC dance education students, including providing the opportunity to create curricula, plan instruction, guide student progress, and lead dance instruction as well as to receive ongoing mentorship and evaluation by peers, DC faculty, and DC students.
- Develop and implement student-centered, self-directed dance curricula that support collaborative problem solving, inquiry-based instruction, 21st-century learning skills, and best practice in dance.
- Support preservice teacher education and the application of innovative instructional strategies to promote innovative instructional methods that can be widely replicated.

Time Span

The project spans the entire year, using the summer months for evaluating the program and planning for the academic year.

Summer

In the summer, DC director and DC coordinator and graduate mentor meet to look over program documentation (photos, journals, and participant evaluations) and to analyze the data collected from the previous year in order to assess and evaluate the program's success. This program review helps the leaders determine what is working and what is not, make small and large changes in the program, and establish scheduling for the following year. At this time, the DC director and coordinator discuss the research focus, curricular initiatives of interest, website and publication status, and upcoming conference presentations.

Fall Semester

In the fall, the DC program coordinator creates flyers advertising the Dancers Connect program. The flyer is mailed to local dance teachers and e-mailed to past participants and teachers and administrators who might have students interested in the program. In early August, the program coordinator and the USC dance education students hold two auditions for the DC program. The audition includes technique class, choreographic problem solving, and discussion components. Once the DC student participants are selected, the DC coordinator meets with their parents to discuss the program, answer questions, and sign a commitment contract. The commitment contract addresses responsibility to themselves and to their group by being on time, being positive and supporting one another's efforts, and always trying their best in all aspects of the class.

Each week, the graduate mentor and three USC students guide the instruction. To balance access, commitment, and leadership, the USC students sign up for specific DC dates they will participate (five sessions per semester are required). Throughout the year the DC program director, DC coordinator and graduate mentor, USC students, and DC students discuss, deliberate, and determine ongoing curriculum based on the interests and needs of participants. This may include curricular content, the calendar of classes and community events such as campus flash mobs, community center performances, site-specific dances, informal sharing, festivals, and workshops.

Spring Semester

The DC program coordinator holds a spring audition in order to add new students to the program. This may happen as a result of word of mouth, recommendations by dance teachers or peers, or participation in other USC community initiatives. In the spring the focus of the DC program and curriculum continues to evolve organically based on the needs and interests of the participants.

The USC dance education program hosts several professional development workshops occurring on Saturdays throughout the year. As members of the dance education community, the DC students receive special access and individualized classes with dance experts. In 2013 USC hosted a community service initiative called Hip Hop for Hope to raise awareness of local and international hunger needs with professional hip-hop dance teachers, graffiti artists, and a DJ on hand. DC students also participated in a reconstruction of Donald McKayle's modern dance masterwork, "Rainbow Round My Shoulder," depicting racial injustice and the violence experienced by prisoners on a chain gang in the South, and an interactive technology program offered by the USC dance education program. At the end of each semester is an informal dance sharing of work for parents and friends where DC students present what they have learned and perform choreography projects.

Assessment

At the end of each semester, USC dance education students are evaluated with the use of a preservice practicum evaluation form. This form is an official record of the students' practicum hours and progress toward student teacher certification. The DC students are evaluated on technical and creative improvement by the DC coordinator, their peers, and themselves. The DC students fill out a personal and a program assessment form identifying successes and challenges they faced. The students' journals also present a record of what they accomplished, learned, and experienced during the year. DC parents fill out a questionnaire identifying their interest, what they saw, and what their children discovered in the program.

In their journals, the DC students discussed their personal growth during the classes, citing the importance of developing relationships with USC students and working collaboratively with students from other schools. One student described how DC has taken her dancing to the next level; others expressed pleasure coming to USC and becoming part of USC campus life.

With feelings of pride and self-satisfaction, the students shared new skills, dances, and experiences with their teachers and peers. A common theme included an awareness of their possibilities in the dance world and the understanding of what a career in dance might look like not only as a performer or choreographer but also as a videographer, scholar, and critic. It is believed that this is a direct result of the personal and professional connections made during the DC classes and the DC curriculum. The DC director and coordinator are encouraged that these middle school students have begun looking seriously at careers and college life and have begun to define themselves as working toward a future as university students. It is believed that by working collaboratively with current university students, the DC students are beginning to see a deeper relationship between the university and the community as a new prospect for themselves.

In their journals, university students addressed the importance of classroom management skills, allocating adequate time for planning, communication with peers, and making personal connections with the DC students, including knowing and using the DC students' names in every class. In addition, the university students expressed that the DC program promoted their personal growth as leaders and teachers. Several students spoke of the importance of taking personal responsibility for the curriculum and how it was presented, resolving challenges as they occurred, providing an opportunity to compare the needs of various students through their instruction and their actions, developing an understanding of students' needs and opening themselves up to forming real relationships, and knowledge of the discipline of dance. They felt that the DC program was a safe opportunity to analyze, discuss, evaluate, and change their own practice of dance instruction. In many cases, participation in the DC program helped preservice teachers begin to develop their own philosophy of dance education.

As a result of the Columbia, South Carolina, community support and successful participation in the Richland One Honors Dance Festival, the DC program has tripled in size and the DC director and program coordinators are considering offering three levels of classes for middle school students, upper elementary students, and freshmen in high school. Table 4.3 presents Parrish's work in Kolb's experiential learning model.

TABLE 4.3   Public Scholarship in Dance Research: Dancers Connect

Kolb's model	Actions	Outcomes
Phase 1 Concrete experiences	University students meet with community partner (middle school students) to discuss needs and read current literature.	University students are oriented to the program and to the associated research project. University students are involved in the development of lessons and assessments.
Phase 2 Observation and reflection	University students apply knowledge in the development of the project.	University students deliver instruction and complete evaluations of their teaching. They complete journal entries of their experiences. The DC students also complete journal entries about their experiences.

(continued)

Table 4.3 *(continued)*

Kolb's model	Actions	Outcomes
Phase 3 Forming abstract concepts	Collaboration continues to develop based on information from literature, community, and faculty. University students conduct research, collect data, and focus on qualitative and quantitative outcomes.	University students are actively involved in data transcription and analysis. Selected students are trained to analyze journal entries for interviews. Changes to curricula are made.
Phase 4 Testing in new situations	Students apply knowledge.	University students apply the lessons learned in their new roles as dance educators or prepare to return to the DC project.
Dissemination	Students create reflective essays, posters, interviews, off-campus presentations, websites, journal articles, dance, drama, visual art, or music expressions.	Students participate in national conference, NDEO 2011. They share what they have learned through the research and engagement process.

CONTEMPORARY DANCE: DAVE THE POTTER (THE LIFE OF DAVID DRAKE IN DANCE, POETRY, AND MUSIC)

Type of Project

Arts-based research

Researchers

Lynnette Young Overby, P. Gabrielle Foreman, Glenis Redmond, Vincent Thomas, Teresa Emmons, Jonathan Green, Ralph Russell, Audrey Wright and the Dancers

University Partners

University of Delaware and Christina Cultural Arts Center

Description of Project

This project is a multidisciplinary interpretation of the life and times of David Drake, Dave the Potter. This was in the late 1800s during slavery in South Carolina and his life as a potter and a man who experienced the satisfaction of mastering a trade accompanied by the inevitable horror of slavery. Following were the goals of the project:

1. Create, perform, and disseminate the story of David Drake through original music, choreography, and poetry inspired by the paintings by Jonathan Green and the historical setting.
2. Inform audiences and students of all ages through the performance and workshops.
3. Create a permanent exhibit of materials through web technology.

Dave the Potter is known for turning large stoneware pots—some large enough to hold up to 40 pounds. Stoneware pots were a common commodity in the mid-1800s and used as containers for meat and meals on plantations. Mastering the ability to create these pots required many years

Vincent Thomas as Dave the Potter.

Photo courtesy of Dan Dunlap.

of training and great skill. He inscribed many of his pots with poetry, a remarkable feat considering he was enslaved and denied the right to read or write. The poetry he inscribed on the pots was simple but direct and often told stories of his times, his family, and his friends. Dave's pots were covered with a unique alkaline glaze that helps researchers identify his pots today, but more important to identification and history, his name and poetic couplets inscribed on them also helped. The following couplet was used as an inspiration for this project:

> *I wonder where is all my relations Friendship to all and every nation*
> *16 August 1857.*

Literacy in antebellum South Carolina, especially within slavery, was rare and at times illegal, which makes Dave's exhibition of his skill even more significant. Some slave owners allowed and even taught their workers to read so that the workers would be able to read the Bible. However, regardless of the extent to which slaves were allowed to read during that time, even fewer were allowed to write. Closer to the Civil War, however, literacy among slaves was almost universally outlawed. Many of Dave's couplets were inscribed right before the Civil War.

Collaborators

The following people collaborated on this project:

- P. Gabrielle Foreman is a literary historian who introduced Dave to the other collaborators.
- Jonathan Green is a world-renowned painter who created a series of paintings on Dave's life in 1998.
- Glenis Redmond is a prolific poet who was inspired by Dave's story, the paintings, and her own South Carolina roots, which enabled her to visualize and create poems that brought Dave's story to life.
- Vincent Thomas, choreographer and native of Edgefield, South Carolina, grew up in the same town as Dave Drake, walked the same paths, and experienced the same South Carolina culture—although over 100 years later. He is Sir Dave in the production.
- Ralph Russell gave the production sound, rhythm, and harmony as he carefully composed and edited music to work with both the theme and the needs of the choreographers.
- Teresa Emmons, a Dover High School dance teacher, created a dance about markets.
- Audrey Wright, undergraduate researcher, provided historical materials for the dancers.

- Jennifer Ferris, graduate student, conducted archival research and created and taught eighth-grade students lessons about slavery and Dave's life.
- Other collaborators included the dancers from the University of Delaware and from Christina Cultural Arts Center.

Process

Multidisciplinary arts-based research takes time, resources, relationship building, and patience. The process evolved over two years and was supported by grants obtained through the University of Delaware Interdisciplinary Humanities Research Center in the fall of 2012. In January 2013, several of the collaborators visited South Carolina to view the pots, visit museums, and gain permission to use the paintings of Jonathan Green as a backdrop and inspiration for the project. Permission was given and the next phase began. The core group of collaborators (choreographer, poet, literary historian, and composer) met to discuss and outline the entire project in August 2013.

During the fall of 2013, auditions were held, choreography was developed and taught, and the poetry and music compositions were completed and integrated into the choreography. The dancers were from the University of Delaware and Christina Cultural Arts Center. The dancers ranged in age from 12 to 50 years.

Photo courtesy of Dan Dunlap.

Creating and teaching the dance "Field Cotton."

During early rehearsals, each dancer was given written information about slavery and was guided in developing a character, an enslaved family member. This character held true throughout the production. Character development was the most important part of the choreography process. The dancers were encouraged to take a part in the choreography and contribute their own ideas and movements. They also created their own personas of a cotton picker to perform on stage. Dancers were given excerpts from striking personal narratives of slaves in order to empathize with the people who lived in the time period by reading their words and learning about their lives.

A story board was created for envisioning the scenes of this dance. The choreographer worked closely with the dancers, encouraging them to remain in character throughout the many hours of rehearsal. The dancers explored the entire process of a day, picking cotton from dawn till dusk. Undergraduate researcher Audrey Wright was able to provide the dancers with narratives and historical information about life as an enslaved person. The resulting choreography was a combination of pantomime and dance and set to the sounds of Russell's music and Redmond's poetry.

The production premiered in March of 2014. It included seven dances plus a musical prelude and postlude, a 40-minute production with live music and poetry. View the production by searching "Dave the Potter" on YouTube.

Assessment

Dave the Potter is an example of arts-based research. The process of creating the production and the production itself promoted a deeper understanding and greater access to the historic topic of slavery by transforming the material into an artistic work. Specific instruments used were observations of performance, rehearsal videos, and audience reflections. Table 4.4 presents Overby's work in Kolb's experiential learning model.

ADDITIONAL COMMUNITY-BASED RESEARCH EXAMPLES

Community-based research methods allow the dance educator to collect contextual data. Careful planning, recording, and analysis of data will provide rich layers of information.

Participatory Action Research

Participatory action research (PAR) strategies involve the participants as co-researchers. Unlike the top-down method, in which the researcher

TABLE 4.4   Public Scholarship in Dance Research: *Dave the Potter*

Kolb's model	Actions	Outcomes
Phase 1 Concrete experiences	Participants read and review historical research. They visit South Carolina. They meet with all collaborators: literary historian, composer, visual artist, poet.	Choreography begins. Poetry is developed. Compositions are developed.
Phase 2 Observation and reflection	Participants apply knowledge in the development of the project.	Dancers take on characters (enslaved families). They begin learning choreography with music and poetry.
Phase 3 Forming abstract concepts	Collaboration continues to develop based on information from literature, community, and faculty.	Dancers, choreographers, poet, literary historian, and composer continue to refine suite of 7 dances.
Phase 4 Testing in new situations	They conduct research, collect data, and focus on qualitative and quantitative outcomes. They apply it in a new situation.	*Dave the Potter* is performed as a complete suite of dances. The suite is presented as a lecture demonstration, an example of arts-based multidisciplinary performance research for national audiences.
Dissemination	Participants perform it and create and maintain website. They give national presentations. They post on YouTube.	Performances: University of Delaware, Wilmington 2014 Website: http://sites.udel.edu/davethepotter National presentations: Council for Undergraduate Research Annual Conference 2014 YouTube: search "Dave the Potter"

functions as one with the knowledge, in PAR the participant is seen as a contributor to the research process. Together the researcher and community partner co-create, co-implement, co-assess, and co-disseminate new knowledge, often designed to solve an existing problem. Photovoice and participatory photo mapping (PPM) are forms of PAR.

PAR is collaborative, critical, participatory, and developmental. It focuses on enabling key stakeholders to address problems they see as important. It is concerned with research alongside stakeholders rather than doing research about them. It links theory and practice and calls for rigorous critical thinking from all involved. PAR aims for ownership of the whole development process by agency stakeholders. It argues that each specific change should be determined by those who will be affected by it.

As an example, Piran (2001) used her long-term involvement with a coeducational residential dance school as the basis for her participatory action research project. In this project, she used focus group methodology to address concerns of body image of adolescent girls. As co-researchers, the girls recognized their own biases regarding size and shape. With recognition came the realization that attitudinal change was needed.

Photovoice

Photovoice is a participatory action research methodology that facilitates participant empowerment by creating and combining photography with grassroots social action. Participants are asked to represent their community point of view by taking photographs, discussing them, developing narratives to go with their photos, and conducting outreach or other action. This research methodology was developed by Caroline C. Wang of the University of Michigan and Mary Ann Burris of the Ford Foundation in 1992.

In teaching students to observe specific movement qualities that may be unique to their community, they are each provided with cameras and instructed to photograph friends or family in various activities, including dancing. The students then view and discuss the photographs together with the teacher or researcher. They observe similarities and differences from various photos and gain an appreciation of their own and others' movement qualities.

Participatory Photo Mapping

Participatory photo mapping, or PPM, is a transdisciplinary community-based research methodology that integrates digital tools, narrative interviewing, and participatory protocols for knowledge production. In this method, community members are provided with digital cameras and GIS units. They take photos of some aspect of their community where change is needed. The photos then become the object of interviews that are attached to particular images. The third step entails a mapping of the images with the GIS data. Finally, action items are developed by the participants and presented to policy makers. This method can engage people in research about their lived experiences. Both qualitative and quantitative data emanate from this methodology.

Community dance programs provide a venue for community-based research methodology involving participatory photo mapping. Here is a research question: If free dance classes are offered as a part of a recreation program in a low-income section of the city, will more middle school girls become involved in and appreciate the benefits of physical activity? Girls, who self-identify as low physical activity, are given the opportunity to take dance classes and research their lived experiences. With partners, the girls take photos of their typical day before participating in the dance classes. Next, their partners photograph them participating in dance classes. Before-and-after photos are used as interview prompts for a discussion about the importance of dance and physical activity. Finally, the girls are told to write letters to the principals of their schools and the local recreation center director, requesting more opportunities to have dance classes. In essence, the girls select photos they believe best represent their lives. They contextualize the photos by telling the story of the photos. They identify what they consider to be the themes that emerge from the photos.

Arts-Based Research

Arts-based research is defined as "an effort to extend beyond the limiting constraints of discursive communication in order to express meanings that otherwise would be ineffable" (Barone and Eisner 2012, p. 1). This is different from research activities in which the arts are used as data for answering a traditional research question (McNiff 2008). Some choreography falls into the realm of arts-based research if it focuses on issues that make a difference in society. This type of arts-based research is connected to community engagement because the choreography grapples with and provides insight into important societal issues. The choreography examples in this book, specifically the work of Gingrasso, Metal-Corbin, and Overby, fit into the category of arts-based research.

WRAP-UP

Community-based research provides participants, faculty, and university students with the opportunity to make significant changes in individuals, the community, and larger policy issues. The data derived from these scholarly activities can also be shared with other researchers—replication is key to promoting long-term institutionalized change in the way dance is viewed in the world.

The examples in this chapter provide specific research questions that guide the project. Although the designs vary from quasi-experimental to ethnographic, the results demonstrate the power of dance to make a difference. Reflective practices occur throughout each project, thus connecting research to Kolb's theory of experiential learning. Dissemination—so important for dance research in becoming a force for change—is showcased in local, national, and international venues as well as in publications. See figure 4.2 for the public scholarship in dance quadrant of research.

The last section of the chapter introduces other community-based research methods that can be used in granting power and authority to the community partners as knowledgeable co-researchers.

FIGURE 4.2   PUBLIC SCHOLARSHIP IN DANCE QUADRANT FOR RESEARCH

High scholarship, low engagement	High scholarship, high engagement
	Giguere Overby (1) Parrish Overby (2)
Low scholarship, low engagement	Low scholarship, high engagement

5

SERVICE

Anybody can be great because anybody can serve.

Martin Luther King, Jr.

Service at times gets a bad reputation in university settings. Providing service to the university, professional, and local and global communities is often viewed as the least worthwhile use of a university professor's time, at least in terms of promotion, tenure, and merit considerations. This is because service has traditionally been an area without clearly defined boundaries. Service can be anything from serving as a committee member at the university to serving as a president of a national disciplinary organization. Teaching (with student and peer evaluations) and research (with peer-reviewed publications) are areas much more easily assessed. In dance, choreography can be reviewed and critiqued by experts. Public scholarship in dance and other disciplines easily crosses boundaries of teaching, research, and service. The assessment of this form of scholarship requires an expansion of what counts (the project) and determination of how the project rises to a level of excellence.

Scholarship Assessed (Glassick, Huber, and Maeroff 1997) provides standards for the many forms of scholarship expressed by Boyer (1990), including teaching, research, application, integration, and service. Reflection occurs in this framework as a dance faculty member plans, implements, and assesses service projects. The following standards are provided for all types of public scholarship, including service:

1. Clear goals: Does the scholar state the basic purposes of his or her work clearly? Does the scholar define objectives that are realistic and achievable? Does the scholar identify important questions in the field?

2. Adequate preparation: Does the scholar show an understanding of existing scholarship in the field? Does the scholar bring the necessary skills to his or her work? Does the scholar bring together the resources necessary for moving the project forward?

3. Appropriate methods: Does the scholar use methods appropriate to the goals? Does the scholar apply effectively the methods selected? Does the scholar modify procedures in response to changing circumstances?

4. Significant results: Does the scholar achieve the goals? Does the scholar's work add significantly to the field? Does the scholar's work open additional areas for further exploration?

5. Effective presentation: Does the scholar use a suitable style and effective organization to present his or her work? Does the scholar use appropriate forums for communicating work to its intended audiences? Does the scholar present his or her message with clarity and integrity?

6. Reflective critique: Does the scholar critically evaluate his or her own work? Does the scholar bring an appropriate breadth of evidence to his or her critique? Does the scholar use evaluation to improve the quality of future work?

These standards can provide dance faculty members with guidance when planning service activities and evaluating these efforts. The examples in this chapter represent the types of service dance faculty are often called on to perform: consulting, leading professional organizations, and professional development.

CONSULTING

University dance educators are often involved in consulting activities that may include creating state and national standards for dance education. Barbara Bashaw from Rutgers is 1 of 10 dance educators nationwide selected in 2011 to develop the national standards that will be used by dance educators in every state.

Clear Goals

The purpose of this project is to develop national dance education standards. Bashaw prepared for the task of creating new dance education standards in the following ways:

- Questioning the gaps and assumptions implicit in existing standards so that scholars are careful about what is continued and progressed into the new standards
- Staying alert to the preferences and biases of the task force group (group-think) as best as possible and entertaining alternatives before decision making
- Reviewing research that sheds light on skills, processes, and learning in dance and bringing that to bear in both the concepts embedded and the scope and sequence of the standards
- Revealing dance experience as embodied cognition and challenging the history of body–mind dualism
- Representing the spectrum of artistry of children as they engage in artistic processes through the varied developmental perspectives
- Representing pedagogical possibility along the educational-to-professional spectrum (Smith-Autard 2002) so that dance educators can find "situatedness" within the new standards and so that they are challenged to nourish dance learners to the fullest extent

- Projecting current educational trends such as key competencies of common core learning, 21st-century skills, and teacher accountability
- Recalling embodied artistry experience as well as teaching experience to both generate and assess content for the standards
- Articulating the multidimensional processes in dance artistry with consideration for how these processes give voice to principles of democracy

Adequate Preparation

Professor Bashaw brings years of teaching, curriculum development, and dance administration to this project:

- She has permanent K-12 dance teacher certification in New York and New Jersey.
- She collaborated with classroom teachers as a teaching artist in dozens of elementary and secondary public schools in New York City through organizations such as ArtsConnection and the Creative Arts Laboratory and the 92Y School Partners program.
- She cofounded the Bridge for Dance studio in New York City.
- She founded the dance program at PS 295, the Studio School for Arts and Culture, a public school in Brooklyn. There she collaborated with the children in creating social justice works and developed a standards-based dance curriculum that also reinterpreted the literacy standards as an embodied frame for dance learning. Her acclaimed Choreographers' Workshop methods and multischool Dance Notation Pen Pal Project have been noted in *Dance Teacher* magazine and *NYC's Best Schools* and featured in resources developed by the Institute for Learning at the University of Pittsburgh.
- From 2002 to 2009 she developed the graduate program in dance education at NYU, including the accredited P-12 dance teacher certification program and the American Ballet Theatre ballet pedagogy program. She was awarded the NYU Steinhardt Teaching Excellence Award in 2009.
- In 2009 she began developing the newly accredited P-12 dance teacher certification program at Rutgers University.
- In New York she has served on the committees developing the dance content exam for teacher certification, the high school

dance exam, the Blueprint for Dance, and the Arts Achieve i3 assessment project. She is a charter member of the New York State Academy for Teaching and Learning and a founding board member of NYSDEA.

- She works closely with the New Jersey Department of Education on career and technical education testing and dance teacher development and is a board member of Dance New Jersey.

Appropriate Methods

Professor Bashaw brings her knowledge of dance pedagogy, current research, and new technologies to the project:

- She is the technology liaison for the dance standards group, running the web meetings and assisting with the project work site. She applies her knowledge of educational technology in developing sample cornerstone assessments that include tasks such as building project websites, WebQuests, and distance-learning projects.

- Barbara's research background includes investigating artistic practice through a human development frame. Understanding the artistic needs of K-12 students from a developmental frame advocates for expanded notions of artistry, or what Bashaw terms a spectrum of artistry (2011). It is important to Bashaw that dance teachers help parents, administrators, and policy makers recognize that children's dancing and dance making be not an incomplete version of adult artistry. It is critical for dance educators to consider how the physical, cognitive, and perceptual abilities that children and adolescents bring to their dance learning may be suited to their cultural context and life phase. These artistic expressions contribute to the artistic horizons of the field.

Significant Results

National grade-level standards, activities, and assessments have been developed. It is expected that these standards will guide the development, implementation, and assessment of dance teaching in K-12 throughout the United States and have a positive global impact.

Effective Presentation

The new National Core Arts Standards are available in print and web-based formats (see table 5.1 for the components of the standards). The material has been presented at local, regional, and national conferences.

TABLE 5.1 National Core Arts Standards: Artistic Processes

Creating	Performing, presenting, producing	Responding	Connecting
Conceiving and developing new artistic ideas and work	**Performing:** Realizing artistic ideas and work through interpretation and presentation **Presenting:** Interpreting and sharing artistic work **Producing:** Realizing and presenting artistic ideas and work	Understanding and evaluating how the arts convey meaning	Relating artistic ideas and work with personal meaning and external context

Reflective Critique

Barbara Bashaw reflects on her work:

> I believe one of the perennial issues we have encountered in the field of dance education has to do with the notion of democracy. Unless an individual is economically and otherwise privileged in this country his or her opportunity to learn in, through, and about dance is quite slim. The inclusion of dance in public education is important for this very reason. But it goes deeper than context. It lies at the very heart of what education means within a democratic society, namely principles of democratic practice that cut across context. For me the call to develop national standards in dance education is a call to renew our commitment to the democratic right of children and all learners best articulated by Jane Bonbright (2007), founding executive director of NDEO:
>
> > . . . [W]e do not rest until ALL students in America have equal opportunity, and access, to high quality dance arts education regardless of gender, age, interest, ability, or culture. Arts education tests the very principles of democracy—freedom to communicate, freedom to experience, freedom to participate, freedom to choose, freedom to explore one's potential, and freedom to be an individual with unique beliefs, interests, and talents—for life. (p. 11)
>
> While we have long laid the blame for the marginalization of dance in education on historical ties to physical education, funding, and educational governance, I believe we also need to understand how we contribute to, consent to, and give reality to this problem though our own actions in the field. In the large picture, the new standards position the arts as a critical aspect of educational prog-

ress for all learners. More intimately, the new standards can point us toward checking that our curricula and teaching practices ensure the fundamental freedoms for students that Bonbright so valiantly articulates. As the dance task force worked on the lattice of the new national standards, these freedoms were at the forefront of our minds. The new national standards in dance therefore also provoke dance artists, educators, administrators, and scholars to consider this question: How well are we doing, and what can we be doing, in terms of ensuring the freedoms described by Bonbright to students, protégés, collaborators, and colleagues?

LEADING PROFESSIONAL ORGANIZATIONS

Dance professionals are often called on to serve in leadership roles for state, national, and international organizations. Ann Kipling Brown has been a leader of Dance and the Child International organization (daCi) since 1982. She served in the following roles:

- 1993 to 2003: treasurer and member of executive committee, daCi advisory committee
- 2003 to 2007: member at large of executive committee, daCi advisory committee
- 2007 to 2010: chairperson of executive committee, daCi advisory committee

Using the standards for scholarly work, Ann describes her work with daCi as a scholarly endeavor. This is especially true in directing the 2000 international daCi conference.

Clear Goals

The purpose of this project is to lead the Dance and the Child International organization.

Adequate Preparation

Ann Kipling Brown describes her start with daCi:

I attended the first conference of daCi in Sweden with Dr. Ann Hutchinson Guest. Ann and I gave a session on the use of the Laban system of notation with children. We worked with children from the Virginia Tanner Children's Dance Theatre, presenting a session with motif writing that I led, and then Ann taught a folk dance using structured notation.

In 1982 I was living in the UK and teaching at the London College of Dance and Drama, working in creative dance, dance pedagogy, choreography, and notation. Subsequent to the Swedish conference I became involved in the design of the UK conference. However, in 1984 I moved to Edmonton to teach in the Alberta Children's Creative Dance Theatre led by Dr. Joyce Boorman and to take up graduate studies.

Dance and the Child International (2000): The Dance Saskatchewan Evening on the University of Regina campus.

It was while in Edmonton that I met Dorothy Harris, a wonderful mentor and friend, who asked me in 1993 to take up the position of treasurer and member of the daCi advisory board. I attended my first advisory board meeting in 1994, chaired by Jean Silver. I held this position until 2003 when I became a member at large.

In 1997 I brought together a group of colleagues from Regina, Saskatchewan, to prepare and present a proposal for a conference to be held in our city. After three years of hard work the daCi 2000 Conference, Extensions and Extremities: Points of Departure, took place successfully on the University of Regina campus. Since 2009 I have been a co-chair representing daCi of the joint summit with the World Dance Alliance and hosted by the Taipei National University of the Arts (TNUA). The daCi/WDA Summit, titled Dance, Young People and Change, was held from July 14 to 20, 2012, at the TNUA School of Dance.

Appropriate Methods

Professor Brown brings her knowledge of dance administration, pedagogy, and current research to her various leadership positions.

Significant Results

Scholarly contributions to service are provided in this section.

- She has served as treasurer and member of daCi. She keeps in touch with members, encourages networking, and promotes the triennial daCi conferences. She keeps records of the daCi finances.
- Her most significant accomplishment is the organization and realization of the daCi 2000 Conference in Regina, Saskatchewan.
- She designed and implemented the daCi website in 2007.
- She assembled previous conference abstracts and papers into an anthology for the study of children's dance: *daCi Anthology* (2012). She has also created the *daCi Reader*, all daCi papers on the daCi website.

Effective Presentation

Materials are presented in web-based format. An international conference provides programming and professional development for children and teachers. Print and online proceedings extend the reach of the conference to children and their teachers throughout the world.

Reflective Critique

Mâmawohkamâtowin, a Cree wording meaning "cooperation; working together toward common goals," reflects the values of a learning and scholarly community that combines innovative thinking and classroom theory with real-world practice. Community involvement has been a primary focus of Kipling Brown's work with students, teachers, and artists.

Kipling Brown reflects:

Since 1982 I have been involved with Dance and the Child International (daCi) as an active member and board member. This association has provided me with the opportunity to collaborate with dance educators from many countries, extending my understanding and practice in dance and teacher education. Focusing on project-based learning that emphasizes learning activities that are long-term, interdisciplinary, student-centered, and integrated with real-world issues and practices, projects have aimed to motivate students by engaging them in their own learning. I have discovered that all participants have enjoyed working together to experience body-based learning; to emphasize learning that becomes more relevant and useful to students; to shape dance experiences for the diverse populations of today's classrooms; to come to understand the power of dance to change attitudes and expectations; and to extend one's abilities to explore and express thoughts, ideas, feelings, and experiences through movement.

PROFESSIONAL DEVELOPMENT

The reality of the lack of dance education opportunities for the majority of elementary school-age students where only 4 percent offer dance as a separate subject, taught by a specialist, prompted Lynnette Young Overby to answer the following question: How can we promote the inclusion of more dance and movement experiences in K-12 education? The answer to the question has taken several forms, including professional development workshops and seminars, independent study course work, oral presentations at conferences, and writing for publication. Overby, professor of theatre and dance at the University of Delaware, worked with the community partner of teachers from schools in Michigan, Delaware, and beyond to aid their professional development. The professional development for K-12 classroom teachers is the focus of this example.

Photo courtesy of Tomaz Crnez Photography.

In-service and preservice teachers enthusiastically engage in dance integration.

Clear Goals

The goal of this work has been to integrate dance into the K-12 curriculum by providing models and guidance in designing, implementing, and assessing arts-integrated lessons.

Adequate Preparation

Staying current with changing educational practices, attendance, and participation in workshops and seminars is very important. A few of the training opportunities follow:

- Train as a Kennedy Center teaching artist: All selected artists participate in annual professional development workshops.
- Train as an adjunct professor with Lesley University in their creative arts and learning master's program.
- Study with Veronica Boix-Mansilla from Harvard University Project Zero, which supports the concept of multiple intelligences.

Appropriate Methods

From 1999 to the present a method of professional development has been in place to guide teachers in their understanding of the dance

elements, the use of local standards, and assessments in the development of these models. Teachers are provided with background knowledge and skills in dance elements and terminology. Then they are
guided in developing arts-integrated lessons that include educational
standards, exploratory and culminating activities, and assessments.
Teachers also participate in lesson study. In this approach, teachers view
and critique lessons by their peers and then teach the same lesson again
for additional feedback. Finally, undergraduate students (ArtsBridge
Scholars) are trained to create, implement, and assess arts-integrated
lessons and become assistants to many of the classroom teachers.

Significant Results

Conducting assessment immediately after the seminars, and in some
cases up to a year later, has a positive impact on the professional development, attitudes, and behavior of teachers. Grant funding to continue
this work has been provided on a regular basis from a variety of funding
sources, including the Michigan Department of Education, the Dana
Foundation, and the National Geography Education Foundation.

Effective Presentation

One book, *Interdisciplinary Learning Through Dance: 101 Moventures*, has
provided guidance to numerous educators throughout the world. Presentations have been given at state, national, and international venues
in multiple formats, from 45-minute sessions to multiyear programs.

A website, www.teacharts.msu.edu/pila, hosts examples of lessons
and assessments. Also, the Program for Interdisciplinary Learning
through the Arts supports the development and sharing of lessons,
reflections, videos, and other resources.

Reflective Critique

Evaluation is a critical component of this work. Assessments occur
immediately after the workshops as well as in the forms of focus groups,
interviews with participants, and final letters written by teachers who
are pursuing graduate degrees. Evaluations have informed Overby's
current and future work with teachers. Overby reflects the following:

> In reflecting on the many years of professional development with
> teachers, it is very clear that the teachers are very open to this type
> of information and that they are extremely busy with the required
> teaching and assessing of core content. I have also found that, once
> teachers realize that not only do the students enjoy the physical activity

and creativity of dance activities but that the dance concepts also link so well with academic content, the students are able to learn both the academic content and the dance skill simultaneously. This is an a-ha moment that changes both the attitude and behaviors of classroom teachers. They become advocates for dance and movement in all forms—and especially as an interdisciplinary connector.

WRAP-UP

Dance educators provide important service to the community in their roles as consultants and leaders of professional organizations and by providing professional development for classroom and other dance educators.

> . . . this approach has the potential to make the campus a more just community, where varying contributions to the institution's mission are better understood and more fairly honored once they are made public and evaluated by the highest standards to which scholars can aspire. (Glassick, Huber, and Maeroff 1997, p. 49)

Glassick and colleagues' standards provide a framework for assessment that enables one to clearly communicate the impact of this form of service. Figure 5.1 applies the criteria from the public scholarship in dance quadrant in chapter 1 to the service quadrant.

FIGURE 5.1   PUBLIC SCHOLARSHIP IN DANCE QUADRANT OF SERVICE

High scholarship, low engagement	High scholarship, high engagement
	Bashaw Kipling Brown Overby
Low scholarship, low engagement	Low scholarship, high engagement

6

ASSESSMENT

Assessment can produce the evidence of impact many faculty require and, thus, can lead to broader participation.

Gelmon, Holland, Driscoll, Spring, and Kerrigan,
Assessing Service-Learning and Civic Engagement

Throughout this book, many examples of assessment are presented in the context of specific programs and projects. Various forms of assessments provide public scholars with materials that can be used for documentation of community engagement projects and for evaluation and revision of current work. Assessment may be formative (occur on a regular basis throughout the project) or summative (occurring only at the end of the project). Assessment is essential for marketing and documenting the project and preparing materials for consideration in promotion, tenure, and merit. This chapter presents descriptions and guidelines of assessments appropriate for public scholarship in teaching, choreography, research, and service.

Assessment is key to providing information for program evaluation and improvement and demonstrating the impact of the project. When selecting and designing assessment instruments, educators and administrators should thoroughly understand the program context and goals. Next, identification of resources in terms of time and personnel is needed. The following questions can help in establishing the beginning of the assessment process (Gelmon et al. 2001):

- What is the aim of the assessment?
- Who wants or needs the information from the assessment?
- What resources are available to support the assessment?
- Who will conduct the assessment?
- How can one ensure the results are used?

Answers to these questions allow the assessment process to fit the specific circumstances involved in the program. The aims will be clearly articulated, and the assessment will take place with appropriate instrumentation and allocation of resources.

ASSESSMENT INSTRUMENTS

Assessment instruments include surveys, interviews and focus groups, journals, e-portfolios, creative reflections, and rubrics. They provide two types of data: qualitative (themes, phrases, observations) and quantitative (numbers, trends, statistics).

Surveys

The survey may be used in assessing attitudes and behavior of all stakeholders in the community engagement project. The format of a survey is usually based on a five-point Likert scale. This scale allows the participant to reveal his or her level of agreement with the statement. The scale ranges from strongly disagree (1) to strongly agree (5). Numerical data are then available for analysis.

Several survey instruments are available through the Internet, including the following: www.surveymonkey.com, www.freeonline-surveys.com, and www.qualtrics.com. Most universities have access to one or more of these services. For example, at the University of Delaware, the online survey tool Qualtrics is available to all members of the university community. The online survey instruments are able to provide descriptive statistics immediately. Survey questions may relate to the participants' perspectives and perceptions on the specific components of the project. For example, choreographers can indicate their perception of the level of connection between the choreography and the community issue. A teacher can assess the impact of the service learning experience on students' future civic engagement goals. In research, the survey can be used in answering a specific research question (e.g., is there a positive impact on the attitudes of school-age students regarding arts-integrated learning experiences?). Here is an example of a question in a service survey: How useful are the dance education standards for developing lessons and assessments? The survey instrument may also be used across projects, at multiple universities, and in a longitudinal approach (i.e., spanning several years).

Interviews and Focus Groups

Interviews and focus groups promote a personal conversation between the project director and the participants. Interviews are one-on-one conversations, while focus groups occur with two or more participants. The focus group interview allows the participants to interact and build on the comments, which may generate more responses. More *why* questions can be answered in this format, and a deeper understanding of the impact of the community engagement activity can be communicated by the participants.

When conducting interviews and focus groups, you need to maintain a structure: Begin on time, explain the goals of the project, take notes or ask permission to record, and use probes (follow-up questions) to deepen the responses. At the conclusion of the process, thank the participants.

Transcribing (writing or typing) the interview or focus groups should occur immediately. By allowing several members of the team to read the transcription, you can generate a list of key words to be coded into specific themes or ideas. These themes will allow the project director to determine attainment of the goal and personal impact of the project. Data analysis may be accomplished with or without the use of a

data analysis package. A few of the data analysis packages are Atlas.
ti, Maxqda, NVivo, QDA Miner, Qualrus, and RQDA.

Journals

Journal writing promotes reflection and may reveal changes in personal, professional, and academic knowledge that result from participation in a community engagement project. The choreographer may
record thoughts in a journal after each rehearsal, the teacher and students may do so after each service learning encounter, the researcher
may write after observing a specific incident that relates to the research
question, and the community participants can write in their journals
after reviewing a product completed during the community engagement activity. In other words, all partners can use journal writing as
a tool for reflection and critical analysis.

A well-written journal prompt accomplishes the following:

- It helps them reflect on what they learned via the creation of the
artifact.
- It connects their learning to desired learning and reflection outcomes.

Here are examples of journal prompts appropriate for a university
student involved in a service project:

- Briefly describe your experience of the community engagement
activity.
- Where were you, what did you do, what were the challenges, and
what did you accomplish?
- How does this experience contribute to the legacy of Dr. Martin
Luther King?
- Select one specific event and respond to the following prompts:
  - Why was it such an important event to you?
  - How did you feel about it?
  - What actions did you take? Is there an action you wish you
  had taken?
  - What is the relationship of this experience to your academic
  objectives?

Rich stories often emerge from journals, and the information may
be useful in augmenting other assessment tools. Journal writing may
move beyond text to include drawings, prose, poetry, and letters to
stakeholders.

Analysis of journals primarily falls within the qualitative assessment arena with transcription and coding of themes. Narrative analysis can also be a tool for gaining meaning because it focuses on stories or accounts (Reissman 2008). Journals may also be viewed quantitatively when entries are categorized and numbers are assigned.

E-Portfolios

As an assessment tool, e-portfolios may provide a place for the collection and showcasing of learning and impact. An e-portfolio may include digital artifacts, reflections of lessons, video clips, poster presentations, hyperlinks, images, and texts. The website may be interactive and include wikis and blogs. A choreographer may post versions of the developing choreography, teachers and students can post lessons and reflections, researchers can incorporate blogs in their journal reflections, and community partners can access the site to support current and future learning. Analysis of e-portfolios can occur with the use of rubrics that include a focus on content and presentation of the multimedia materials.

Creative Reflections

Reflections can take many forms as long as the outcomes are clearly connected to the reflective activity. Some exciting forms of reflection are writing poetry, music lyrics, and personal essays and, of course, creating choreography.

Rubrics

Rubrics provide both guidance in developing projects and criteria for assessing projects. For example, the arts integration rubric (see figure A.10) provides guidance for the development and assessment of arts-integrated curricula. The Leaps for Language Movement assessment developed for a lesson with preschool students focuses on specific dance skills (see figure A.11). The community engagement rubric contains specific criteria for the development and assessment of community engagement projects (see figure A.12). This rubric was based on the definition of the Carnegie Foundation for the Advancement of Teaching. Community engagement describes collaboration between institutions of higher education and their larger communities (local, regional/state, national, global) for the mutually beneficial exchange of knowledge and resources in a context of partnership and reciprocity (http://nerche.org/index.php?option=com_content&view =article&id=341&Itemid=92).

PROJECT DEVELOPMENT: THE LOGIC MODEL

The logic model is used for planning, implementation, and assessment of various types of projects. It is also a useful communication device. The parts of the model include inputs (resources, contributions, and investments that go into the program); outputs (activities, services, events, and products); and outcomes (results or changes that are expected for individuals, groups, communities, or organizations). An example of a logic model appears in table 6.1.

TABLE 6.1   Logic Model for University of Delaware Arts Education Grant Project

Inputs	Outputs	Outcomes
Staff	Assess knowledge base needs in target population of youth.	Determine baseline levels of knowledge and awareness in target population.
Federal granting agency funds	Assess awareness of need for arts education in target population and supporting groups (e.g., community, faculty, local boards).	Collaborate in production of multidisciplinary instructional materials.
School district facilities	Provide interdisciplinary team training to participating teachers throughout the duration of the project.	Increase artistic knowledge and awareness of participating teachers.
School district financial support	Design interdisciplinary units of instruction appropriate to the educational level of a middle school student population and based on methods, technology, materials, and skills available for project.	Increase artistic knowledge and skills of target population.
Delaware Department of Education support	Continuous formative assessment of program design.	Increase over time in number of students receiving multidisciplinary instruction in functionally related topics.
University of Delaware research facilities	Disseminate program results throughout home district schools in Delaware.	Over time increase numbers of instructional units available to practicing educators in Delaware and nationwide.

Inputs	Outputs	Outcomes
School district faculty partici-pation	Establish measureable and valid indices of growth and progress in student achieve-ment and program effective-ness.	Increase educators' teaching effectiveness.
UD arts education undergraduate research participation	Set specific and rational crite-ria for student success.	Broaden educators' appre-ciation for interrelationships among many topics and skill sets.

RESPONSIBLE CONDUCT OF RESEARCH

Each university has an office that provides training, application guide-lines, and decisions on work with human participants. The university office of research or office of compliance is an important resource for gaining approval to conduct any form of data collection that involves human participants. Many school systems also have offices that over-see research projects. Assessing student learning through interviews, observations, and journal writing may require permission from parents and an assent (verbal or written agreement) from K-12 students.

Appropriate training is often a requirement. This training entails several online sessions that provide background information about appropriate procedures for the conduct of research with humans.

WRAP-UP

Assessment instruments provide information that is useful when devel-oping, implementing, and evaluating all forms of public scholarship: teaching, choreography, research, and service. The use of multiple forms of assessment, including surveys, interviews, e-portfolios, and reflective journal writing, provides qualitative and quantitative infor-mation. By including both formative (ongoing) and summative (final) assessments, data from the project will yield information that will be helpful in determining the impact of the project.

7

FINAL THOUGHTS

Expand what counts. Document what counts. Present what counts. Expand who counts.

Ellison and Eatman, *Scholarship in Public*

Throughout this book, successful dance professors share examples of their work that extend beyond the classroom or studio. The college or university mission includes teaching, research, creative activities, and service. The dance faculty profiled in this book demonstrate that by engaging the community in their work; the impact is integrated in all university missions (see figure 7.1). This is especially true of public scholarship that blurs the lines in teaching, service, and research as scholarship. This integration becomes clearer if we consider a specific example.

While teaching a modern dance technique class, the instructor includes a service learning component (teaching). The students and faculty member contact a Girls and Boys Club in the community. Together they discuss the needs of the children who attend the club. It is determined that the children would benefit from a program that focuses on gaining a deeper understanding of themselves. The students researched the topic, then created dance activities, including choreography designed to focus on developing self-understanding. The faculty member developed pre- and postassessments in collaboration with a statistics instructor. The university students taught the lessons and then reflected on their deepening understanding of teaching and working with young people.

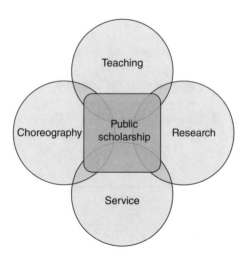

Figure 7.1 Public scholarship encompassing the university missions of teaching, research, creative activities (choreography), and service.

In this example, we see the overlap of teaching, research, choreography, and service that may occur simultaneously in a public scholarship project.

Kolb's theory of experiential learning provides a framework for exploration of the learning that occurs during the creative process of teaching, choreography, research, and service. Furthermore, the examples give us insight into the process from the point of view of the dance faculty member and, in some cases, the students and community members.

The service examples are embedded in the assessment guidelines developed by Glassick and colleagues (1997), which provide a structure for both planning and evaluation of scholarly service.

The public scholarship in dance quadrant allows us to view public scholarship on a continuum from low engagement and low scholarship to high engagement and high scholarship while recognizing that the project could move from one level to another depending on planning and allocation of time and resources.

Mutually beneficial partnerships are the keystone of public scholarship. Everyone wins—university students, community partners, universities, and dance faculty members (see figure 7.2).

Mutually Beneficial Partnerships

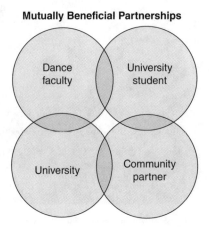

Figure 7.2 Everyone wins with mutually beneficial partnerships.

TEACHING

Academic service learning is the most researched form of public engagement. There is strong support of the benefits, especially for student engagement and retention. The importance of reflection cannot be too strongly emphasized; this is the link between the receipt of information and deep knowing through application and reflection.

CHOREOGRAPHY

A strong interdisciplinary focus occurs when choreography becomes the vehicle for expression of a community need. Whether it is personal (stories of the people) or curricular (based on fifth-grade history), the choreography becomes more than a personal artistic expression—it fills a void in the community and artistic world.

Earl Robbins/fotolia.com

In public scholarship, choreography can become community expression, not just a personal artistic expression.

RESEARCH

The field of dance needs much more research. By incorporating a community focus, we involve many more partners in the research process—the students (undergraduate and graduate) and the community partners. Even though many dance faculty are stretched to the limit with responsibilities of choreography, teaching, and university service, they are also very involved with community issues and concerns. With a focus on community engagement, researchers are no longer the faculty members working alone in the library, lab, or studio. By using participatory action research, Photovoice, arts-based research, and additional qualitative and quantitative methods, dance educators have tools to support scholarly work that is also beneficial to community partners. The entire field of dance will benefit from this approach to knowledge acquisition.

SERVICE

Dance faculty in higher education will always be the servant leaders of the profession but with a focus on public scholarship. The service can also count as scholarly activity. By expanding who counts (the public) and expanding what counts (documents, curricula, standards), the work is no longer something to do on the side but rather a task that is meaningful to all partners and counts toward promotion, tenure, and merit increases.

Public scholarship is here to stay. In fact, it has the potential to become a 21st-century answer to student engagement, faculty motivation, and global citizenship. The examples and resources in this text will allow current and future dance educators to view their work as one piece of a puzzle that involves the wisdom of many.

APPENDIX

APPENDIX A.1 TEACHING: CHECKLIST FOR HIGH ENGAGEMENT, HIGH SCHOLARSHIP

Community Engagement
- ❏ Identify community needs.
- ❏ Establish long-term relationship with partner.
- ❏ Include community partner in the development of curricular content that reflects community partners' expectations of student learning outcomes.

Student Outcomes
- ❏ Include engagement goals in planning.
- ❏ Provide students with information about the community partner.
- ❏ Provide students with knowledge of life-span development and pedagogy skills.

Academic Connections
- ❏ Include academic content that connects with community need.
- ❏ Include clear connection to principles of community engagement.
- ❏ Include clear connection to students' professional goals.

Assessment Strategies
- ❏ Include academic content assessments.
- ❏ Include community partner assessments.
- ❏ Include community engagement and service assessments.

Dissemination Goals
- ❏ Present locally, nationally, or internationally with all partners.
- ❏ Publish lesson plans on a website.
- ❏ Publish with all partners.

From L. Overby, 2016, *Public Scholarship in Dance* (Champaign, IL: Human Kinetics).

APPENDIX A.2   SERVICE: CHECKLIST FOR HIGH ENGAGEMENT, HIGH SCHOLARSHIP

Community Engagement

❏ Identify community needs.

❏ Establish long-term relationship with partner.

❏ Include community partner in the development of service project.

Disciplinary Connections

❏ Focus on disciplinary content that connects with community need.

❏ Establish clear connection to principles of community engagement.

❏ Establish clear connection to faculty members' professional goals.

Research and Assessment Methods

❏ Use logic model for planning, implementation, and assessment.

❏ Apply other qualitative, quantitative, or mixed methods.

Dissemination Goals

❏ Present data or project locally, nationally, or internationally with all partners.

❏ Distribute findings through the Internet.

❏ Prepare publications with contributions by all partners.

From L. Overby, 2016, *Public Scholarship in Dance* (Champaign, IL: Human Kinetics).

APPENDIX A.3 CHOREOGRAPHY: CHECKLIST FOR HIGH ENGAGEMENT, HIGH SCHOLARSHIP

Community Engagement
❏ Identify community needs.

❏ Establish long-term relationship with partner.

❏ Include community partner in the development of choreography.

Disciplinary Connections
❏ Focus on disciplinary content that connects with community need.

❏ Connect choreography with principles of community engagement.

❏ Maintain clear connection to faculty members' professional goals.

Assessment
❏ Assess artistic outcomes (choreography and performance).

❏ Assess dancers' and audience members' civic and personal outcomes.

❏ Use a variety of assessment tools: survey, observation, journal writing, and so on.

Dancer Outcomes
❏ Include engagement goals in planning.

❏ Provide dancers with information about the community partner and issue.

❏ Provide dancers with the opportunity to improvise or co-create choreography.

Dissemination Goals
❏ Present in local, national, or international venue.

❏ Post on YouTube.

❏ Publish process.

From L. Overby, 2016, *Public Scholarship in Dance* (Champaign, IL: Human Kinetics).

APPENDIX A.4   RESEARCH:
CHECKLIST FOR HIGH ENGAGEMENT,
HIGH SCHOLARSHIP

Community Engagement

❏ Identify community needs.

❏ Establish long-term relationship with partner.

❏ Include community partner in all aspects of research.

Disciplinary Connections

❏ Focus on disciplinary content that connects with community need.

❏ Connect research questions with principles of community engagement.

❏ Maintain clear connection to faculty members' professional goals.

Research Methodology

❏ Gain permission to conduct research from institutional research board.

❏ Use a variety of research tools (qualitative and quantitative).

❏ Include community partner as a co-researcher.

Dissemination Goals

❏ Co-present in local, national, or international venues.

❏ Publish research in disciplinary and practical journals.

From L. Overby, 2016, *Public Scholarship in Dance* (Champaign, IL: Human Kinetics).

APPENDIX A.5   POSTCOURSE STUDENT SURVEY

Teaching Methods in Physical Education I/Teaching Movement Education

[Instructor's name here]

Please respond to the following questions in detail and with honesty. The instructor will use this information in improving the course in the future.

1. What was the *most* relevant, meaningful content and what were the most relevant and meaningful activities in this course?

2. What was the *least* relevant, meaningful content and what were the least relevant and meaningful activities in this course?

3. In what ways could this course be improved (e.g., changes in content, course design or organization, assignments and projects, evaluation: any additions or deletions)? Please give *specific* suggestions.

4. On a scale of 1 to 5 (1 = low, 5 = high), rate your level of confidence (e.g., comfort, competence) as a *mover* (i.e., your ability to move and participate in a variety of physical activities).

1	2	3	4	5
Not at all confident	Not confident	Uncertain	Confident	Totally confident

5. On a scale of 1 to 5 (1 = low, 5 = high), rate your level of confidence (e.g., comfort, competence) as a *movement education teacher*.

1	2	3	4	5
Not at all confident	Not confident	Uncertain	Confident	Totally confident

6. To what degree do you feel prepared to teach movement to elementary children? What would help you to feel more prepared?

7. Any additional comments?

Name _____
[Instructor's name here]

From L. Overby, 2016, *Public Scholarship in Dance* (Champaign, IL: Human Kinetics).

APPENDIX A.6 PARENT EVALUATION SURVEY OF HOMESCHOOL PHYSICAL EDUCATION PROGRAM

Please return to the registration desk before you leave today.

Parents: We would appreciate your input regarding this term's physical education lessons for your children. Your ideas will provide the student teachers with feedback about their teaching as well as help us to make this experience as good as possible for your children in the future. All comments, suggestions, and ideas (both positive and constructive) are encouraged and welcome. Thank you!

1. We have tried to provide the children with a wide range of movement and physical activities this term. We used a different theme each week, including fitness, creative movement, fundamental motor skills, dance and rhythms, gymnastics, and games. What were your impressions of the physical activities that were taught this term? Which were your and your children's favorites and least favorites?

2. Describe any movements and activities, use of equipment and music, space and environmental factors, or teaching methods and practices that you thought were unsafe or inappropriate for a particular age group (or for individuals). What would you suggest the students improve so that all content and teaching methods are developmentally appropriate?

3. What were your overall impressions of the student teachers' abilities to organize, manage, teach, and interact with your children? What did they do well? How could they improve?

4. How did the Friday morning time work for your schedule? Next term, the class will meet on Tuesday and Thursday mornings; in the spring term, the classes will meet on Tuesday and Thursday afternoons. Will these days and times work for your schedule? What other days and times would work well for you?

5. How did you and your children like the length of the lessons (i.e., 60 minutes)? Was it long enough or too long?

6. How did the location of the NPE gym (and upper gymnastics room) and stadium parking area work for you? Was it convenient?

7. What is the best way to communicate with you? State your preference: e-mail, Yahoo.com WOU PE Homeschool PE Group site, or other means.

8. What worked well this term? What should we continue to do the same way?

9. What didn't work well this term? How can we improve the program? What should we do differently?

10. Can you think of anything that we could add to the program to make it better?

11. Any additional comments?

Thank you! We hope to see you next term.

From L. Overby, 2016, *Public Scholarship in Dance* (Champaign, IL: Human Kinetics).

APPENDIX A.7   SAMPLE E-MAIL TO HOST TEACHER

Dear Ms. _____:

Thank you for agreeing to be a host teacher for our DANC 497 Teaching Movement in the Schools practicum. We are _____ [name] and _____ [name] and we are [arts ed/music pedagogy/dance] majors at UM.

Our professor, [name], has asked us to schedule four classes in November, approximately 30 minutes each. Each of us will teach two classes and will support the other when they teach. We are interested in using creative movement to reinforce your curriculum, so we will ask you for some curricular information next month.

For now, we would like to set the teaching schedule. We have the following times available for teaching. Can you schedule us during these days and times in 30-minute blocks? If not, please suggest some other days or times and we will see if we can arrange it with our classes.

[Times listed]

Thank you in advance for hosting us. We look forward to meeting you and your students.

Sincerely, _____

From L. Overby, 2016, *Public Scholarship in Dance* (Champaign, IL: Human Kinetics).

APPENDIX A.8 INTEGRATED DANCE LESSON PLANNING GUIDE

Teacher and Dancer Planning Sheet

Title of content area _____ Teaching date _____

1. What is the target learning? (What do you want the children to know or be able to do after the lesson?)
2. What is the specific vocabulary used in this unit?
3. What do the students already know?
4. Will these themes and learning targets be used in only one lesson or spread out over several lessons?
5. Additional information. (Are there particular ways you would teach this concept? Are there follow-up lessons you may be doing?)

Integrated Dance Lesson Plan: Dancing the Rainforest by Karen Kaufmann

Dance	Other content area
1. What is my art target learning? What do I want my students to know and be able to do in dance? Example: Students move at a variety of levels. **2. What will be the evidence of student learning?** Example: Students will demonstrate moving at *high-middle-low levels* in the lesson exploration and final group choreography.	**What is my shared target learning?** What do I want my students to know and be able to do? Example: Students relate 4 levels of the rainforest (floor, understory, canopy, emergent layer) to levels in space. **What will be the evidence of student learning?** Example: Students will use low, middle, and high levels, and action words, to demonstrate the differences between the emergent, canopy, understory, and ground levels of the rainforest.

Lesson components
1. Warm-up
Guide students through stretching, bending, twisting, and shaking actions to get the blood and breath moving and mobilize joints and muscles.
Lead the Brain Dance to integrate body and mind.

(continued)

2. Introduce your dance target learning and its enduring understanding.

Example: Today we'll be working on low, middle, and high levels. Our special words today are *low, middle,* and *high.*

Write it on the board and demonstrate the three levels using dance. Ask questions. Explain its importance in the world. ("Everything in the world moves at a specific level or uses more than one level.")

3. Movement exploration *(This contains your written prompts)*

Explore your target learning (high, medium high, medium low, low) in a variety of contexts, with a range of stimulus words, using the movement elements *(body parts, shapes, directions, pathways, tempos, movement qualities, relationships, and so on).*

Formative assessment: Room scan with reverse checklist.

4. Introduce your combined target learning

Example: "Today we'll be using movement to demonstrate our understanding of the four levels of the rainforest *and* the levels at which the body moves. As you've studied in class, the rainforest has . . ."

5. Lesson core *(This contains your written prompts)*

Lead your students in an activity that builds skills in the shared target learnings.

Emergent level: **very high + jumping and reaching**

Canopy level: **medium high + darting wide**

Understory level: **medium low + creeping fast and slow**

Forest floor: **low + slowly rolling and settling**

Repeat and reinforce the synthesis of the dance and curricular material in multiple ways: from movement to rainforest vocabulary and rainforest vocabulary to movement vocabulary.

Formative assessment: Can students dance the four levels of the rainforest? Can they connect the movement to the rainforest level? Can they connect the rainforest level to the movement?

Criteria-based partner critique or room scan with reverse checklist by teachers.

6. Culminating activity (summative assessment)

Lead your students through a final activity that demonstrates their learning. Example: Divide class into groups of 3 or 4 and ask each group to choose 2 or 3 levels of the rainforest to demonstrate in their dance. Give time to develop.

Ask each group to tell the class which two they have chosen (i.e., emergent and understory). Watch the dance performed. Viewers are asked to assess by holding up their fingers (4-3-2-1) indicating whether the group demonstrated their two levels appropriately.

Peer assessment criteria (written on a chart):

4: Levels and actions in the dance clearly depict the rainforest level.

3: Level and action almost always clearly depict the rainforest level.

2: Only some of the level and action clearly depict the rainforest level.

1: The level and action don't depict the rainforest level.

Summative assessment: Criteria-based peer critique, teacher-based checklist, or analytic rubric or journal reflection.

7. Reflection and review

Lead your students through a reflection process. Reflect on the following:

a. Raise your hand if you can name three levels we use in space.

b. Raise your hand if you can name one of the four levels of the rainforest.

c. Raise your hand if you can tell me a time you used one of the levels at home or on the playground or in your classroom. "I used a _____ level when I _____."

d. Raise your hand if you can think of a place that has all the levels in space contained within it.

From L. Overby, 2016, *Public Scholarship in Dance* (Champaign, IL: Human Kinetics).

APPENDIX A.9   CLASSROOM OBSERVATION FORM

Visit your teaching site the week before you start teaching and observe for at least one hour. This is your baseline experience for the service learning project. Be specific. Type a minimum of two pages, double-spaced, to include in your service learning portfolio.

Write an in-depth observation of the following:

- **The students:** What do you observe about them? Their bodies? Their intellect? Their attention span? Their relationships with one another? What do you sense about them?
- **Classroom environment:** How much space is in the room? How is it filled? How is the room used?
- **Curriculum:** What is being taught? How is it being taught? Are the students getting it?
- **Teacher's style:** How does the teacher interact with students? How would you describe the teaching style?
- **Verbal and nonverbal communication:** How does the teacher communicate?
- **Classroom management:** Do you see any techniques being used?
- Now that you've seen the students, teacher, and space, what will you take into consideration when you plan your classes?

From L. Overby, 2016, *Public Scholarship in Dance* (Champaign, IL: Human Kinetics).

APPENDIX A.10   ARTS INTEGRATION RUBRIC

Score	0	1	2	3	4
Theme	Students demonstrate no understanding of theme. All memorizing and reciting knowledge.	Students demonstrate very little knowledge of the theme. Mostly memorizing and reciting knowledge.	Students demonstrate some knowledge of the theme. Mostly memorizing and reciting knowledge.	Students are mostly engaged in constructing and demonstrating understanding of the theme. Some memorizing and reciting knowledge.	Students are fully engaged in constructing and demonstrating understanding of the theme. Very little memorizing or reciting of knowledge.
Art form	Students do not construct or demonstrate their understanding of the art form.	Students seem unsure of their art form and do not have a complete understanding.	Students seem as if they have an understanding of the art form but have difficulty demonstrating it by themselves.	Students have full understanding of the art form and are engaged in constructing and demonstrating their art form with some assistance.	Students have full understanding of the art form and are engaged in constructing and demonstrating their art form without any assistance.
Creative process	Students did not create any original work. Engaged in copying work. Students did not share products.	Students created some original work, but mostly engaged in copying.	Students created mostly original work, but engaged in some copying.	Students were engaged in the process of creating original work, but relied heavily on other works.	Students were engaged in the process of creating original work and created all work on their own. Students shared products.

(continued)

Arts Integration Rubric *(continued)*

Score	0	1	2	3	4
Con-nection	No con-nection between the art form and theme. The theme does not rein-force the art form.	Small focus on the theme, but no connec-tion, and the theme does not reinforce the art form.	Some con-nection between the art form and the theme. The theme somewhat reinforces the art form.	Largely focused on connection between the art form and theme. The theme somewhat reinforces the art form.	Clear con-nection between the art form and the theme. Theme enhances the art form.

From L. Overby, 2016, *Public Scholarship in Dance* (Champaign, IL: Human Kinetics).

APPENDIX A.11   LEAPS FOR LANGUAGE MOVEMENT ASSESSMENT PRE- AND POSTTEST

Score	1	2	3
Self-space	Touches friends all the time, does not follow directions or spread out.	Touches friends some of the time, spreads out initially but then moves back in.	Never touches friends. Spreads out and stays in own bubble.
Pathways	Seems confused about concept. Either stands or doesn't move in the right pathway.	May be confused and follows friends at first, but moves correctly 50% of the time.	Moves in the correct pathway without following friends.
Levels	Seems confused about concept. Either stands or does not move in the correct level.	May be confused and follows friends at first, but moves correctly 50% of the time.	Moves in the correct level without following friends.
Shapes	Seems confused about concept. Does not make a shape at all.	May be confused and follows friends at first, but tries to make a shape.	Makes a shape without following friends.
Creativity	Stands or does not participate most of the time.	Is actively engaged even though he or she may not understand.	Actively engaged, coming up with creative movement patterns and shapes.

From L. Overby, 2016, *Public Scholarship in Dance* (Champaign, IL: Human Kinetics). This rubric was developed by ArtsBridge Scholar Julie Luzier as an assessment for students who participated in her Leaps for Learning project.

APPENDIX A.12   COMMUNITY ENGAGEMENT RUBRIC— FROM OUTREACH TO ENGAGEMENT

	Low level of community engagement	Mid level of community engagement	High level of community engagement
Identifying shared interests, potential partners, and possible projects	• Project is designed primarily by one partner, with little input from the other partner(s).	• The project emerges in a context of knowledge of all partners' interests, needs, and abilities. • Partner involvement may be intermittent, unequal, incomplete, or unsatisfactory.	• Project emerges in context of mutual interest, needs, and abilities. • Partners are actively involved in all aspects of the collaboration—from identifying participants to design, implementation, dissemination, and continuation of the project.
Establishing a plan that fulfills community and university interests	• One partner addresses the project's objectives, timetable, and mode of communication, but there is little dialogue with the other partner about leadership and work roles, or equitable allocation of time or other resources. • Issues of trust and responsibility are lacking.	• Partners consider the project's objectives, timetable, and mode of communication, but may not have a formal agreement about leadership and work roles, equitable allocation of time and other resources. • Issues of trust, information flows, and responsibility are unclear.	• Partners have a clear understanding of the project's objectives, timetable, and mode of communication. • Partners have determined an equitable allocation of time and resources. • Partners may have a formal agreement about leadership and work roles. • Issues of trust, information, and responsibility are balanced.

	Low level of community engagement	Mid level of community engagement	High level of community engagement
Fostering reciprocity and mutual recognition	• Partners have little discussion about how the project's objectives, implementation process, and outcomes fulfill the wishes of either partner. • Efforts to ensure reciprocity, mutual recognition, and reward are nonexistent.	• Partners intermittently discuss whether the project's objectives, implementation process, and outcomes are meeting the needs of each partner. • Efforts to ensure reciprocity, mutual recognition, and reward are not clearly articulated.	• Partners have ongoing in-depth discussions to consider whether the project's objectives, processes, outcomes are meeting the needs of each partner. • Efforts to ensure reciprocity, mutual recognition, and reward are ongoing.
Assessment guides decision making about projects	• No assessment process is in place.	• Formative and summative assessment process is informal and inconsistent.	• A formalized formative and summative assessment process exists and guides decisions about current and future project development.
Laying the foundations for continued engagement and dissemination of outcomes	• Partners have no plan to deepen or expand project, except on a one-time or short-term level. • No dissemination plans exist.	• Partners informally discuss next steps for continued engagement. However, one or both partners may not be fully committed to continuing partnership. • The dissemination process is informal.	• Partners formally and informally consider ways to improve, initiate changes that will strengthen levels of reciprocity and mutual reward, and actively acknowledge and support the value of the partnership. • Partners formally disseminate project outcomes.

From L. Overby, 2016, *Public Scholarship in Dance* (Champaign, IL: Human Kinetics). This rubric was developed by the University of Delaware Community Engagement Commission. Designed by April Venness, Sue Serra, and Lynnette Overby.

BIBLIOGRAPHY

ArtsEdge. "What is Arts Integration?" Accessed March 8, 2012. http://artsedge. kennedy-center.org/educators/how-to/arts-integration-beta/what-is-arts-integration-beta.aspx.

Aud, S.,W. Hussar, G. Kena, K. Bianco, L. Frohlich, J. Kemp, and K. Tahan. 2011. *The condition of education 2011* (NCES 2011-033). U.S. Department of Education, National Center for Education Statistics. Washington, DC: U.S. Government Printing Office.

Baker, T.A., and C.C. Wang. 2006. Photovoice: Use of a participatory action research method to explore the chronic pain experience of older adults. *Qualitative Health Research* 16(10): 1405-1413. doi:10.11771104973230629411 8.

Banks, S.P., E. Louie, and M. Einerson. 2000. Constructing personal identities in holiday letters. *Journal of Social & Personal Relationships* 17: 299-397. http:// spr.sagepub.com.

Barone, T., and E. Eisner. 2012. *Arts based research*. Los Angeles: Sage.

Bashaw, B. 2011. *Young choreographers: An ethno-phenomenological study of developmental and socio-cultural influences during untutored dance making*. Teachers College, Columbia University, 369.

Bloomgarden, A., and K. O'Meara. 2007. Harmony or cacophony? Faculty role integration and community engagement. *Michigan Journal of Community Service Learning* 13(2): 5-18. In N. Nicotera, N. Cutforth, N. Fretz, and S.S. Thompson, *A higher education conundrum*. 2011. *Journal of Community Engagement and Scholarship* 4 (1): 37-49.

Bonbright, J. 2000/2007. *National agenda for dance arts education: The evolution of dance as an art form intersects with the evolution of federal interest in, and support of, arts education*. NDEO Dancing in the Millennium Conference, Washington, DC.

Boyer, E. 1990. *Scholarship reconsidered priorities of the professoriate*. Princeton, NJ: Carnegie Foundation for the Advancement of Teaching.

Boyer, E. 1996. The scholarship of engagement. *Journal of Public Service and Outreach* 1(1): 11-20.

Brown, R. 2006. *Outreach and engagement continuum*. Unpublished chart, Office of the Associate Provost for University Outreach and Engagement. East Lansing: Michigan State University.

Campus Compact. 2000. President's declaration on the civic responsibility of higher education. www.compact.org/wp-content/uploads/2009/02/Presidents-Declaration.pdf.

Cantor, N. 2010. Imagining America in public life. Paper presented at Imagining America in Public Life annual conference, Seattle.

Chatterton, P., D. Fuller, and P. Routledge. 2007. Relating action to activism: Theoretical and methodological reflections. In *Participatory action research approaches and methods: Connecting people, participation and place,* edited by S.L. Kindon, R. Pain, and M. Kesby. London: Routledge.

Coppin State University Dance Program. Bravo! Dance outreach partnership program. Accessed March 21, 2015. www.coppin.edu/bravodance

Dennis, S.F., S. Gaulocher, R.M. Carpiano, and D. Brown. 2009. Participatory photo mapping (PPM): Exploring an integrated method for health and place research with young people. *Health & Place* 15: 466-473.

Dirks, A. 1996. Organization of knowledge: The emergence of academic specialty in America. http://webhost.bridgew.edu/adirks/ald/papers/orgknow.htm.

Ellison, J., and T.K. Eatman. 2008. *Scholarship in public: Knowledge creation and tenure policy in the engaged university.* Syracuse, NY: Imagining America.

Experiential learning (Kolb). N.d. www.learning-theories.com/experiential-learning-kolb.html.

Fitzgerald, H.E. 2010. Across the higher education landscape. In *Handbook of engaged scholarship contemporary landscapes, future directions: Vol. 1. Institutional change,* edited by H. Fitzgerald, C. Burack, and S. Seifer. East Lansing: Michigan State University Press.

Fitzgerald, M. 2008. Community dance: Dance Arizona Repertory Theatre as a vehicle for cultural emancipation. In *Dance, human rights, and social justice,* edited by N. Jackson and T. Shapiro-Phim. Lanham, MD: Scarecrow Press.

Gelmon, S.B., B.A. Holland, A. Driscoll, A. Spring, and S. Kerrigan. 2001. *Assessing service-learning and civic engagement.* Providence: Campus Compact.

Glass, C.R., and H.E. Fitzgerald. 2010. Engaged scholarship: Historical roots, contemporary challenges. In *Handbook of engaged scholarship contemporary landscapes, future directions: Vol. 1. Institutional change,* edited by H. Fitzgerald, C. Burack, and S. Seifer. East Lansing: Michigan State University Press.

Glassick, C.E., M.T. Huber, and G.I. Maeroff. 1997. *Scholarship assessed: Evaluation of the professoriate.* San Francisco: Jossey-Bass.

Hartley, M. 2012. An engagement for democracy. In *Civic provocations,* edited by D. Harward. Washington, DC: Bringing Theory to Practice.

Hartley, M., and I. Harkavy. 2010. Engaged scholarship and the urban university. In *Handbook of engaged scholarship contemporary landscapes, future directions: Vol. 1. Institutional change,* edited by H. Fitzgerald, C. Burack, and S. Seifer. East Lansing: Michigan State University Press.

James, A. 2008. Participatory action research video presentation. http://doctoratelife.blogspot.com/2008/03/participatory-action-research-video.html.

Kindon, S.L., R. Pain, and M. Kesby. 2007. *Participatory action research approaches and methods: Connecting people, participation and place.* London: Routledge.

Kolb, D.A. 1984. *Experiential learning: Experience as the source of learning and development.* Englewood Cliffs, NJ: Prentice Hall.

Kuh, G. 2008. Why integration and engagement are essential to effective educational practice in the twenty-first century. *Peer Review.* Washington, DC: Association of American Colleges & Universities.

Lerman, L. 2011. *Hiking the horizontal.* Middletown, CT: Wesleyan University Press.

Magruder, E. 2013. *Dancing for young audiences.* Jefferson, NC: McFarland.

Martin, F. 1986. Phenomenography: A research approach investigating different understandings of reality. *Journal of Thought* 21: 28-49.

McIntyre, A. 2008. *Participatory action research.* Los Angeles: Sage.

McNiff, S. 2008. Art-based research. In *Handbook for the arts in qualitative research,* edited by J. Knowles and A.L. Cole. Thousand Oaks, CA: Sage.

New England Resource Center for Higher Education. (2004). http://nerche.org.

Overby, L. 2000, March. The gift of dance: A synthesis of community and university partnerships. National Dance Association Scholar/Artist lecture. Paper presented at the annual convention of the American Alliance for Health, Physical Education, Recreation and Dance, Orlando, FL.

Overby, L. 2004. Integrating dance and drama into the classroom: A research/outreach model, International Conference for Physical Educators. Proceedings (ICPE 2004).

Overby, L. 2005. The voices of teachers: The impact of professional development on the interdisciplinary teaching of dance. In *Dance: Current selected research volume 5,* edited by L. Overby and B. Lepczyk. New York AMS Press.

Overby, L. 2014. Jazz dance as a gateway to community engagement. In *Jazz dance,* edited by L. Guarino and W. Oliver. Gainesville: University Press of Florida.

Overby, L., H. Beach, P. Glassman, R. Scholtz, T. Thomas, and Y. Hernandez. 2013. InterArts, interdisciplinary curricula. *Journal of Dance Education* 13(1): 23-29.

Overby, L., B. Post, and D. Newman. 2005. *Interdisciplinary learning through dance: 101 Moventures.* Champaign, IL: Human Kinetics.

Overby, L., I. Tucker, and T. Terry-Todd. 1992. Survey of dance education in historically black institutions. Paper presented at the annual convention of the Eastern District Association—American Alliance for Health, Physical Education, Recreation and Dance, Baltimore.

Piran, N. 2001. Re-inhabiting the body from the inside out: Girls transform their school environment. In *From subjects to subjectivities: A handbook of interpretive and participatory methods,* edited by D. Tolman and M. Brydon-Miller. New York: New York University Press.

Reason, P., and H. Bradbury. 2001. *Handbook of action research: Participative inquiry and practice.* London: Sage.

Reed, B. 2006. Phenomenography as a way to research the understanding by students of technical concepts. Núcleo de Pesquisa em Tecnologia da Arquitetura e Urbanismo (NUTAU): Technological Innovation and Sustainability. Sao Paulo, Brazil, 1-11.

Reissman, C.K. 2008. *Narrative inquiry: Experience and story in qualitative research.* San Francisco: Jossey-Bass.

Seifer, S.D., and K. Conners, eds. 2007. *Faculty toolkit for service-learning in higher education: Community campus partnerships for health.* Scotts Valley, CA: National Service Learning Clearing House.

Silverstein, L.B., and S. Layne. 2010. What is arts integration? Explore the Kennedy Center's comprehensive definition. The Kennedy Center: ArtsEdge—The National Arts and Education Network. www.kennedy-center.org/education/partners/defining_arts_integration.pdf.

Smith-Autard, J.M. 2002. *The art of dance in education* (2nd ed.). London: Black.

Strand, K., S. Marullo, N. Cutforth, R. Stoecker, and P. Donohue. 2003. *Community-based research and higher education: Principles and practices.* San Francisco: Jossey-Bass.

Turesky, E.F., and D.R. Wood. 2010. Kolb's experiential learning as a critical frame for reflective practice. *Academic Leadership* 8(3): 116-129.

Wang, C.C. 1999. Photovoice: A participatory action research strategy application to women's health. *Journal of Women's Health* 8(2): 185-192.

Wang, C.C., and C.A. Pies. 2004. Family, maternal and child health through Photovoice. *Maternal and Child Health Journal* 8(2): 95-102.

Ward, K., and T. Moore. 2007. Faculty at work: The practice of engaged scholarship. Presentation at Michigan State University, East Lansing.

RESOURCES

Many resources support the work of public scholars. Resources include national organizations with a commitment to community engagement, websites, books, journals, and assessment strategies. This information is useful for many reasons, including program evaluation, assessment of impact, project design, and implementation. Resources come in many forms: books, journals, websites, organizations, and individuals. Accessing these resources will support the work of public scholars in dance throughout their careers.

COMMUNITY ENGAGEMENT ORGANIZATIONS AND CONFERENCES

Engagement Scholarship Consortium Annual Conference
The Engagement Scholarship Consortium (ESC) is a 501(c)(3) non-profit educational organization composed of higher education member institutions, a mix of state, public, and private institutions. The goal of the consortium is to work collaboratively to build strong partnerships between universities and communities that are anchored in the rigor of scholarship and help build community capacity. The website is www.engagementscholarship.org.

Imagining America: Artists and Scholars in Public Life
The mission of Imagining America (IA) is to create democratic spaces that foster and advance publicly engaged scholarship that draws on arts, humanities, and design. The organization catalyzes change in campus practices, structures, and policies that enables artists and scholars to thrive and contribute to community action and revitalization. The organization is a consortium of member universities. The website is www.imaginingamerica.org.

International Association for Research on Service Learning and Community Engagement
This organization focuses on facilitating information exchange and dialogue among scholars, practitioners, funders, and students interested in research on service learning. The website is www.researchslce.org.

International Partnership for Service Learning and Leadership (IPSL)
IPSL programs combine academic studies and community service and full cultural immersion to give students a deeper, more meaningful experience studying abroad. The website is www.ipsl.org.

WEBSITES

Community–Campus Partnerships for Health
The mission of Community–Campus Partnerships for Health is to promote health equity and social justice through partnerships between communities and academic institutions. The website is http://ccph. memberclicks.net.

Scholarship of Engagement
The Clearinghouse for the Scholarship of Engagement sponsors the National Review Board for the Scholarship of Engagement to provide external peer review and evaluation of faculty scholarship of engagement and provide consultation, training, and technical assistance to campuses who are seeking to develop or strengthen systems in support of the scholarship of engagement. The website is www. scholarshipofengagement.org.

Community-Based Collaboratives Research Consortium
CBCRC is a network of researchers, mediators, government agencies, community groups, and environmental groups that seek to understand and assess local collaborative efforts involving natural resources and community development. The website is http://cbcrc.org.

Global Alliance on Community-Engaged Research
The main objective of the alliance is to facilitate the sharing of knowledge and information across continents and countries to enable interaction and collaboration to further the application and impact of community-based research for a sustainable and just future for the people of the world. Organizations involved in community-based research are invited to participate in an open and democratic alliance that adds value to existing networking and collaborative endeavors. The website is www.uvic.ca/research/centres/cue/networks/gacer/index.php.

National Coordinating Centre for Public Engagement in Higher Education
Based in Bush House in central Bristol, England, the National Coordinating Centre for Public Engagement (NCCPE) was established in 2008 as part of the Beacons for Public Engagement Initiative. Funded by the four UK Funding Councils, Research Councils UK and the Wellcome Trust the NCCPE help inspire and support universities to engage with the public. The centre is hosted between the University of Bristol and the University of the West of England. The website is www.publicengagement.ac.uk.

Talloires Network

This is an international association of institutions committed to strengthening the civic roles and social responsibilities of higher education. They work together to implement the recommendations of the Talloires Declaration and build a global movement of engaged universities. The website is http://talloiresnetwork.tufts.edu.

GENERAL RESOURCES ON COMMUNITY ENGAGEMENT

Campus Compact

Campus Compact is a national organization of more than 1,100 college and university presidents who are committed to fulfilling the public purpose of higher education. Campus Compact supports student and faculty involvement in the community. The website includes resources, publications, and conferences: www.compact.org.

PUBLICATION OUTLETS

Michigan Journal of Community Service Learning
This is a national peer-reviewed journal focused on curriculum-based service learning, community-based research, campus–community partnerships, and faculty-engaged (public) scholarship: http://ginsberg.umich.edu/mjcsl.

Journal of Community Engagement and Scholarship
JCES is a peer-reviewed international journal through which faculty, staff, students, and community partners disseminate scholarly works. JCES integrates teaching, research, and community engagement in all disciplines, addressing critical problems identified through a community-participatory process: http://jces.ua.edu.

Public: A Journal of Imagining America
Public is a peer-reviewed, multimedia e-journal focused on humanities, arts, and design in public life: http://public.imaginingamerica.org.

GRANT WRITING

How to Write an Outreach Grant Proposal

This article provides guidelines for developing a successful community engagement proposal: http://chronicle.com/article/How-to-Write-an-Outreach-Gr/46879.

RESOURCES ON PROMOTION, TENURE, AND MERIT

Imagining America: Artists and Scholars in Public Life Tenure Team Initiative on Public Scholarship
The Tenure Team Initiative (TTI), one of the consortium's most important initiatives to date, seeks to articulate and support the adventurous work of publicly engaged scholars and artists: http://imaginingamerica. org/fg-item/scholarship-in-public-knowledge-creation-and-tenure-policy-in-the-engaged-university/?parent=442.

Community–Campus Partnerships for Health's Community-Engaged Scholarship Toolkit
The toolkit is a resource for community-engaged faculty on making their best case for promotion and tenure. More than a dozen recently promoted and tenured faculty members have graciously donated excerpts from their portfolios for posting on the toolkit: https://ccph. memberclicks.net/ces-toolkit.

Community-Engaged Scholarship Review, Promotion & Tenure (RPT) Package
This resource helps RPT committees understand community-engaged scholarship and how to assess its quality and impact: http://depts. washington.edu/ccph/pdf_files/CES_RPT_Package.pdf.

Fitzgerald, H., C. Barack, and S. Seiner. 2011. *Handbook of engaged scholarship, Volume 1: Institutional change; Volume 2: Community-campus partnerships.* Lansing: Michigan State University Press.

Foster, K.M. 2010. Taking a stand: Community-engaged scholarship on the tenure track. *Journal of Community Engagement and Scholarship* 3(2): 20-30. http://jces.ua.edu/taking-a-stand-community-engaged-scholarship-on-the-tenure-track.

Franz, N.K. 2011. Tips for constructing a promotion and tenure dossier that documents engaged scholarship endeavors. *Journal of Higher Education Outreach and Engagement* 15(3): 15-29. http://openjournals.libs.uga.edu/index.php/jheoe/article/view/571.

Glass, C., D. Doberneck, and J. Schweitzer. 2008. Outreach and engagement in promotion and tenure. National Center for the Study of University Engagement, Michigan State University poster. http://ncsue.msu.edu/files/OutreachEngagementPromotionTenure.pdf and http://ncsue.msu.edu/files/PT_Poster.pdf.

O'Meara, K.A. 2001. Working paper No. 25 Scholarship unbound: Assessing service as scholarship in promotion and tenure. New England Resource Center for Higher Education (NERCHE). www.nerche.org/index.php?option=com_content&view=article&id=48&Itemid=38.

Report of the UNC taskforce on future promotion and tenure policies and practices. 2009. University of North Carolina 1-25. http://provost.unc.edu/files/2012/10/Taskforce-on-Future-Promotion-and-Tenure-Policies-and-Practices-FINAL-REPORT-5-8-09.pdf

Seifer, S.D., L.W. Blanchard, C. Jordan, S. Gelmon, and P. McGinley. 2012. Faculty for the engaged campus: Advancing community-engaged careers in the academy. *Journal of Higher Education Outreach and Engagement* 16(1): 5-19. http://openjournals.libs.uga.edu/index.php/jheoe/article/view/747.

Vogelgesang, L.J., N. Denson, and U.M. Jayakumar. 2010. What determines faculty-engaged scholarship? *The Review of Higher Education* 33(4): 437-472.

RESOURCES FOR TEACHING ASSESSMENT

Arter, J., and J. McTighe. 2001. *Scoring rubrics in the classroom.* Thousand Oaks, CA: Corwin Press.

Davies, A. 2007. *Making classroom assessment work.* Courtenay, BC: Connections Pub.

Johnson, E., and J. Jenkins. 2009. Formative and summative assessment. www.education.com/reference/article/formative-and-summative-assessment.

NAEYC. 2008. Accreditation standards—literacy. www.teacherquicksource.com/preschool/3.aspx.

ASSESSMENT WEBSITES

American Evaluation Association: www.eval.org.

ERIC Clearinghouse on Assessment and Evaluation: http://ericae.net.

Free Resources for Program Evaluation and Social Research Methods. http://gsociology.icaap.org/methods.

ABOUT THE AUTHOR

Lynnette Young Overby, PhD, has been a dance educator for more than 30 years. Currently she is a professor of theater and dance at the University of Delaware and chair of the Community Engagement Commission. She was associate dean for outreach and engagement at Michigan State University and a fellow of the Michigan Campus Compact. She also has served as a national teaching artist for the Kennedy Center since 2004.

Dr. Overby is the author or editor of 11 dance education and dance research books. Her work has earned her many awards and honors, including the 2000 Scholar Artist Award from the National Dance Association and the 2004 Leadership Award from the National Dance Education Organization. She earned a PhD in motor development from the University of Maryland, a master's degree in dance education from George Washington University, and a bachelor's degree from Hampton Institute.

CONTRIBUTOR LIST

Chapter 2
Miriam Giguere, Drexel University, Philadelphia, Pennsylvania
Marita Cardinal, Western Oregon University, Monmouth
Karen Kaufmann, University of Montana at Missoula

Chapter 3
Susan Gingrasso, University of Wisconsin at Stevens Point (emeritus)
Ella Magruder, Sweet Briar College, Virginia
Mark Magruder, Sweet Briar College, Virginia
Josie Metal-Corbin, University of Nebraska at Omaha
Lynnette Young Overby, University of Delaware at Newark

Chapter 4
Miriam Giguere, Drexel University, Philadelphia, Pennsylvania
Lynnette Young Overby, University of Delaware at Newark
Mila Parrish, University of North Carolina at Greensboro

Chapter 5
Barbara Bashaw, Rutgers University, New Brunswick, New Jersey
Ann Kipling Brown, University of Regina, Saskatchewan, Canada (emeritus)
Lynnette Young Overby, University of Delaware at Newark

You'll find other outstanding
dance resources at
www.HumanKinetics.com